# Naturally Peninsula
# Flavours

# *Naturally Peninsula*
# Flavours

## PENINSULA
MERCHANDISING LIMITED

# Foreword

The philosophy I try to follow both in my life and in my Sydney restaurant, Billy Kwong, is "to give back to the community, in whatever way I can, whenever I possibly can". Serving the healthiest, freshest, life-giving food is one great way that Billy Kwong can simultaneously inspire people and make a real contribution to their health and happiness.

For a business to have strength in its day-to-day running and clarity of vision in its future, it must have a sense of purpose, a spiritual backbone. The Peninsula Hotels are inspirational in this respect. Apart from the sheer luxury, comfort, flawless service and impeccable attention to detail I have always experienced at The Peninsula Hotels, the reason I keep coming back is their adherence to a philosophy that emphasises wellness and balance.

*Naturally Peninsula – Flavours* is the first cookbook to emerge from the kitchens of the seven Peninsula Hotels throughout Asia and the USA, and it is a true reflection of their guiding principle: "to live well is to eat well".

Fortunately, due to the multitude of health issues confronting our modern society, we are becoming more and more mindful of what we ingest — of what we feed our minds, our bodies and our souls. This book is a tribute to The Peninsula Hotels' dedication to total wellness of being and spirit, and their understanding that, in a very real sense, "we are what we eat".

Each of these recipes demonstrates The Peninsula Hotels' devotion to the finer things in life. When it comes to dining, this means a commitment to the best produce, showcasing the talents of its innovative chefs who employ a diverse range of culinary styles and techniques to bring out the full natural flavour of each and every ingredient.

Similarly, when my chefs and I create dishes for my restaurant, our main aim is to allow the integrity of the ingredients to shine through. Rather than trying to reinvent the wheel, the key is to approach our art with restraint and discipline. If you are dealing with the highest-quality produce, you do not need to do much in order for a dish to really sing.

For me as a chef, experiencing new taste sensations on my travels is a constant source of inspiration. Wherever I find myself, The Peninsula Hotels help me to accomplish this and make the most of new places and experiences.

After using several of these recipes, you will discover for yourself how successfully the Peninsula chefs have united today's healthy-eating principles with the memorable meals offered in their hotels — and you will be able to relive the experience at home.

Kylie Kwong
Chef and Restaurateur

# Introduction

New cooking techniques, new ingredients, new approaches to food — multi-faceted culinary worlds are revealed layer by layer in the 76 recipes of *Naturally Peninsula – Flavours*, the first cookbook to be created by the kitchens of The Peninsula Hotels from its seven properties around the globe.

An emphasis on wellness and balance is the common thread that runs through all the recipes in the book; each *Naturally Peninsula* dish highlights its own unique and pristine flavours while showcasing a range of contemporary culinary techniques which embody today's healthy food principles.

The chefs helming the kitchens at The Peninsula Hotels were given the task to create recipes for *Naturally Peninsula – Flavours*, focusing on the quality and freshness of the ingredients while offering innovative ideas to prepare them with panache. In composing an interesting selection of light and healthy *Naturally Peninsula* dishes, the greatest challenge was to marry lively flavour combinations with creative cooking methods that also preserved the integrity of the ingredients.

Responding from the depths of their creative souls and bringing with them the cultural influences of each Peninsula Hotel destination, the chefs rose majestically to meet this challenge, with passion, style, and a genuine sense of pride in all that The Peninsula Hotels represent — ultimate comfort and service excellence, and an unfailing commitment to deliver a unique and compelling experience to their guests.

*Naturally Peninsula – Flavours* captures the essence of the *Naturally Peninsula* cuisine philosophy together with the energy, imagination and pure talent of the Peninsula chefs, distilling it into 76 tantalising recipes that will enable you to recreate the *Naturally Peninsula* dining experience at home.

The collection of dishes and recipes in this book will inspire anyone who appreciates the vivid, fresh flavours that come from quality ingredients prepared with respect and creativity. While you may find yourself at times grappling with certain cooking techniques and ingredients, the book will take you on a gourmet journey of discovery around the world, opening new epicurean vistas and offering new culinary heights to reach. From cooking techniques such as the poaching of meat in a vacuum bag and the extraction of chlorophyll from parsley leaves, to exotic ingredients such as kohlrabi, kaffir lime leaves, quinoa, Ancho chillies, Chinese wolfberries and Thai rosella, you will experience a growing sense of wonder and accomplishment as you discover and learn to use new cooking techniques and lesser-known culinary treasures.

In essence, *Naturally Peninsula – Flavours* is all about a fresh and modern approach to food. It reflects the *Naturally Peninsula* philosophy of living well by eating well. Continue your journey of total wellness from the luxurious and pampering environment of The Peninsula Hotels' restaurants to the comfort of your own kitchen and home.

Violet Oon
Singapore's Food Ambassador

# Appetisers

Intensely flavoured, served in small portions, and oftentimes the best manifestation of a chef's creative impulses, an appetiser whets your anticipation for the exciting meal ahead. The following repertoire of eight *Naturally Peninsula* appetisers will eagerly open the palate door, teasing and delighting your taste buds with its wide range of flavours and textures. From the imaginative intricacies of the Lightly-Jellied Essence of Tomato with its Own Mousse and Sorbet to the delectable Salad of Tataki Bonito with Spring Onion, Nori and Ponzu, to the more gutsy Corn Nut-Crusted Short Ribs, you will no doubt be spoilt for choice as you decide on the dish with which to debut your meal.

## Snapper Ceviche with Tostones
Preparation Time: 40 minutes   Cooking Time: 10 minutes   Serves 4

### CEVICHE

**Snapper** *1, about 1 kg (2 lb 3 oz), skinned and filleted*

**Fresh or pickled green jalapeno** *1, cut into fine julienne*

**Red onions** *100 g (3¹/₂ oz), peeled and cut into fine julienne*

**Coriander leaves (cilantro)** *a handful, stalks discarded and leaves finely chopped*

**Young ginger** *15 g (¹/₂ oz), peeled and finely chopped*

**Celery** *2 stalks, cut into fine julienne*

**Lime juice** *500 ml (16 fl oz / 2 cups)*

**Fine salt** *1¹/₂ tsp*

**Freshly ground black pepper** *¹/₂ tsp*

### MARINATED CAPSICUMS

**Red, yellow and green capsicums (bell peppers)** *1 each, cored and seeded*

**Lime juice** *2 Tbsp*

**Fine salt** *¹/₄ tsp*

**Ground black pepper** *¹/₄ tsp*

### TOSTONES

**Ripe plantains or semi-ripe bananas** *700 g (1¹/₂ lb)*

**Vegetable oil** *100 ml (3¹/₃ fl oz)*

Prepare ceviche. Thinly slice snapper fillets, then place in a bowl with jalapeno, red onions, coriander, ginger and celery. Toss lightly to mix. Add lime juice to cover fish and marinate for 10–20 minutes until colour of fish changes. Season with salt and pepper. Drain and serve immediately with some of the vegetables in the marinade or store refrigerated, covered with plastic wrap (cling film) until ready to serve. Ceviche should be served within 1 hour of marinating.

Prepare capsicums. Cut into long and fine strips. Place strips into ice water to curl them. When ready, drain and pat dry. Toss with lime juice, salt and pepper. Set aside.

Prepare tostones. Peel and slice plantain or banana into 1-cm (¹/₂-in) thick rounds. Heat oil in a pan and fry plantain or banana rounds for about 4 minutes until tender. Once tender, remove from pan and gently flatten between absorbent paper. Return to hot oil and fry until crisp on the outside.

Serve ceviche with capsicums and tostones. Garnish as desired.

# Salad of Tataki Bonito with Spring Onion, Nori and Ponzu

Preparation Time: 20 minutes   Cooking Time: 5 minutes   Serves 4

### TUNA

Tuna fillet *280 g (10 oz), cut into 4 pieces*

Fine salt *¼ tsp*

Ground black pepper *¼ tsp*

Olive oil *½ tsp*

### PONZU SAUCE

Rice vinegar *3 Tbsp*

Light soy sauce *3 Tbsp*

Mirin *2 Tbsp*

Dried bonito flakes *10 g (⅓ oz)*

Lemon juice *from 1 lemon*

### JAPANESE SALAD

Spring onions (scallions) *55 g (2 oz), cut into fine julienne*

Pickled daikon (white radish) *55 g (2 oz), cut into fine julienne*

Shiitake mushrooms *45 g (1½ oz), cut into fine julienne*

### GARNISH

Dried seaweed (nori) *1 sheet, toasted and cut into fine julienne*

White sesame seeds *1 tsp, toasted*

*Shichimi togarashi* to taste

**NOTE**

Mirin is a sweet, golden-coloured wine made from glutinous rice. It has a low alcohol content and is used to flavour many Japanese dishes and sauces.

*Shichimi togarashi* is usually made up of seven spices. These can include chilli powder, black pepper, sesame seeds, dried mandarin orange peel, seaweed flakes, prickly ash pods, hemp or poppy seeds.

Season tuna with salt and pepper.

In a very hot shallow non-stick frying pan, heat olive oil and quickly colour tuna on all sides for about 20 seconds each. Tuna should still be rare inside. Slice just before serving.

Combine ingredients for *ponzu* sauce in a saucepan and bring to a boil. Remove from heat and strain through a fine sieve. Leave to cool.

Combine ingredients for Japanese salad and season lightly with some ponzu sauce.

Glaze tuna with remaining *ponzu* sauce and serve with Japanese salad. Garnish with seaweed, sesame seeds *and shichimi togarashi.*

# Wild Mushroom Fregola, White Bean Bruschetta and Ratatouille Salad

Start preparations 1 day ahead   Cooking Time: 2 hours 30 minutes   Serves 4

## MUSHROOM FREGOLA

**Shallots** *15 g (¹/₂ oz), peeled and chopped*

**Garlic** *1 clove, peeled and chopped*

**Olive oil** *3 Tbsp*

**Wild mushrooms** *100 g (3¹/₂ oz), stalks discarded, caps chopped*

**Couscous (see Glossary)** *85 g (3 oz)*

**Vegetable stock (see pg 170)** *125 ml (4 fl oz / ¹/₂ cup)*

**Fine salt** *¹/₄ tsp*

**Freshly ground black pepper** *¹/₈ tsp*

## WHITE BEAN BRUSCHETTA

**Dried white beans** *140 g (5 oz), soaked overnight and drained*

**Vegetable stock (see pg 170)** *1.5 litres (48 fl oz / 6 cups)*

**Garlic** *1 clove, peeled*

**Fine salt** *¹/₂ tsp*

**Ground black pepper** *¹/₂ tsp*

**French baguette** *4 slices, each 1.5-cm (³/₄-in) thick*

**Tomatoes** *2 large, peeled (see Note on pg 39), seeded and diced*

**Basil leaves** *1 sprig, chopped*

**Olive oil** *2 Tbsp*

## RATATOUILLE SALAD

**Herb or other flavoured oils** *2 Tbsp*

**Garlic** *1 clove, peeled and chopped*

**Onion** *30 g (1 oz), peeled and chopped*

**Aubergine (eggplant)** *30 g (1 oz), diced*

**Courgette (zucchini)** *30 g (1 oz), diced*

**Red capsicum (bell pepper)** *30 g (1 oz), diced*

**Tomatoes** *2 large, peeled, seeded and diced*

**Fine salt** *¹/₄ tsp*

**Freshly ground black pepper** *¹/₄ tsp*

**Tomato juice** *125 ml (4 fl oz / ¹/₂ cup)*

**Basil leaves** *1 sprig, finely shredded*

**NOTE**

Make up your own flavoured oils using your favourite herbs and spices. Try basil, bay leaves, chervil, dill, fennel, lavender, majoram, mint, parsley, sage and thyme. You can also add peeled cloves of garlic, chillies and peppercorns of various colours, allspice and juniper berries and strips of orange or lemon peel. Clean and air-dry the herbs and spices before using. Place into a clear glass bottle and fill with extra virgin olive oil. Leave in a cool dark place for 4–6 weeks. If making basil oil, first pound the basil leaves using a pestle and mortar to release its oils.

To sweat foods means to cook over gentle heat, covered or partly covered. This way, the food softens and cooks in its own juices without browning.

Prepare mushroom fregola. Sweat chopped shallots and garlic in olive oil over medium heat. Add chopped mushrooms and sweat until tender. Add couscous and cook for 2 minutes until golden.

Add stock and bring to a boil, then lower heat and simmer for 4 –5 minutes until liquid is absorbed, stirring constantly. Season with salt and pepper and mix well. Cover and leave to infuse. When couscous is plumped up, it is ready. Set aside.

Prepare white bean bruschetta. Cook beans in vegetable stock until soft and tender. Takes about 2 hours. Drain, reserving a little stock. Blend half the beans with garlic until smooth. Add reserved stock to make it into a smooth paste. Season with half the salt and pepper.

Grill baguette slices and spread with bean paste.

Mix tomatoes with remaining whole beans and season with remaining salt and pepper. Add chopped basil and olive oil. Spoon onto baguette slices and set aside.

Prepare ratatouille salad. Heat herb oil and sweat garlic over medium heat. Add onion and sweat for 2 minutes. Add aubergine and sweat for 4 minutes. Add courgette and sweat for 3 minutes. Add capsicum and tomatoes and season with salt and pepper. Cook for another 4 minutes, then add tomato juice and cook until reduced. Set aside.

Serve mushroom fregola with white bean bruschetta and ratatouille salad topped with shredded basil. Garnish as desired.

*Photograph on pg 18–19*

## Lightly-Jellied Essence of Tomato with its Own Mousse and Sorbet

Start preparations 1½ days ahead   Cooking Time: 1 hour 15 minutes

Sorbet Freezing Time: 6 hours or until firm by hand; 30–40 minutes using an ice cream machine   Serves 4

### TOMATO ESSENCE

Very ripe cherry tomatoes *900 g (2 lb),
  cut into 1.5-cm (³/₄-in) cubes*

Celery *30 g (1 oz), cut into 1.5-cm (³/₄-in) cubes*

Shallots *10 g (¹/₃ oz), peeled and cut into
  1.5-cm (³/₄-in) cubes*

Fennel bulb (see Glossary) *45 g (1¹/₂ oz), cut
  into 1.5-cm (³/₄-in) cubes*

Garlic *2 cloves, peeled and finely sliced*

Thyme *2 sprigs*

Tarragon *1 sprig*

Basil leaves *10*

Sugar *¹/₂ tsp*

Fine salt *³/₄ tsp*

Ground black pepper *¹/₄ tsp*

Cayenne pepper *¹/₈ tsp*

Tabasco sauce *6 drops*

Worcestershire sauce *5 drops*

### TOMATO JELLY

Gelatine sheets *2 leaves, softened in
  ice water*

Tomato essence *400 ml (13 fl oz)*

### TOMATO MOUSSE

Gelatine sheet *1 leaf, softened in ice water*

Tomato essence *180 ml (6 fl oz / ³/₄ cup)*

### TOMATO SORBET

Olive oil *5 tsp*

White onion *30 g (1 oz), peeled and diced*

Garlic *1 clove, peeled and chopped*

Thyme *1 sprig*

Bay leaf *1*

Tomato paste *70 g (2¹/₂ oz)*

Very ripe tomatoes *280 g (10 oz), chopped*

Basil *1 sprig*

Fine salt *¹/₄ tsp*

Ground black pepper *¹/₈ tsp*

Sugar *30 g (1 oz)*

Vodka *1 Tbsp*

### BASIL PURÉE

Basil leaves *55 g (2 oz)*

Olive oil *60 ml (2 fl oz / ¹/₄ cup)*

Fine salt *¹/₄ tsp*

Ground black pepper *¹/₈ tsp*

Ascorbic acid *¹/₈ tsp*

### TOMATO CHIPS

Tomato *1, cut into thin slices*

### GARNISH

Basil leaves *4 small sprigs*

Balsamic vinegar *2 Tbsp*

Ripe plum (Roma) tomatoes *3, large,
  peeled (see Note on pg 39), seeded
  and cut into 1-cm (¹/₂-in) cubes*

**NOTE**
The ascorbic acid in the basil purée prevents the basil leaves from turning grey. If ascorbic acid is unavailable, blanch basil leaves briefly and drain well before using. Unfortunately, blanching will cause the leaves to lose some flavour.

Combine ingredients for tomato essence and leave for 3 hours. Liquidise into a smooth paste with a blender (food processor). Pour purée into a small muslin bag and hang over a bowl to collect essence. Leave to drip until pulp is completely dry. Check seasoning and adjust to taste.

Prepare tomato jelly. Squeeze softened gelatine sheets of excess water and dissolve in a saucepan over low heat with a little tomato essence. Remove from heat and add remaining essence. Divide jelly among 4 soup plates and refrigerate until firm.

Prepare tomato mousse. Squeeze softened gelatine sheet of excess water and dissolve in a saucepan over low heat with a little tomato essence. Remove from heat and add remaining essence. Pour into a mixing bowl and refrigerate to set. Once set, whisk and pour into a siphon. Leave refrigerated until needed.

Prepare tomato sorbet. Heat olive oil and sweat onion over medium heat until tender. Add garlic, thyme and bay leaf and sweat for another 10 minutes. Add tomato paste and cook for another 10 minutes. Add fresh tomatoes and simmer for 40 minutes. Season to taste then add basil and remove from heat. Allow sauce to stand for 2 hours. Remove herbs and strain liquid through a fine mesh sieve. Adjust seasoning if necessary, add vodka and refrigerate to chill before churning in an ice cream machine according to the manufacturer's instructions. Alternatively, freeze mixture for about 2 hours or until semi-set. Remove from freezer and beat mixture using a cake mixer until mixture is well churned. Return to freezer for another 30 minutes–1 hour, then beat again until well churned. Repeat until sorbet is light.

Prepare basil purée. Combine ingredients and blend (process) into a smooth paste.

Prepare tomato chips. Lay tomato slices on a non-stick baking tray or silicon sheet. Bake in a pre-heated oven at 80°C (176°F) for 6–7 hours until tomato slices are crisp.

Remove jellied soup from refrigerator and serve with sorbet and mousse. Garnish with tomato chips, basil, balsamic vinegar, basil purée and tomato dice. Serve immediately.

*Photograph on pg 22–23*

## Chicken Breast Slices Poached in Lemon and Thyme with Asparagus, Cherry Tomato Confit and Olives

Preparation Time: 45 minutes   Cooking Time: 30 minutes   Serves 4

### CHICKEN

Free-range skinless chicken breast
   *280 g (10 oz)*

Fine salt *¹/₄–¹/₂ tsp*

Ground black pepper *¹/₄ tsp*

Lemon zest *from 1 lemon*

Thyme *3 sprigs*

Chicken stock (see pg 171) *90 ml (3 fl oz / 6 Tbsp)*

### CHERRY TOMATOES

Vine-ripened cherry tomatoes *4, each cut in half*

Olive oil *3 Tbsp*

Garlic *1 clove, peeled and sliced*

Thyme *1 sprig or ¹/₂ tsp dried thyme*

### ASPARAGUS

Water *1 litre (32 fl oz / 1 cup), mixed with 1 tsp salt*

Green asparagus *6 spears*

### ARTICHOKES

Baby artichokes *2*

Ice water *500 ml (16 fl oz / 2 cups)*

Lemon juice *from 1 lemon*

Fine salt *1¹/₈ tsp*

Olive oil *1 tsp*

Ground black pepper *¹/₈ tsp*

### GARNISH

Black Taggiashe olives *15 g (¹/₂ oz)*

Thyme *4 sprigs*

**NOTE**

Confit is a culinary term that describes a cooking method where the ingredients are cooked very slowly in a medium-hot syrup or oil.

Poaching is a method of cooking where the ingredient is cooked in boiling or simmering liquid.

Prepare chicken. Season chicken breast with salt, pepper and lemon zest. Place into a vacuum bag or thick plastic bag with thyme and chicken stock (see Kitchen Techniques).

Heat a pot of water to 70°C (155°F). Place a steaming rack in pot and place bag on it so bag does not come in direct contact with base of pot. Alternatively, clip bag to side of pot. Poach chicken, uncovered, for 16–20 minutes, maintaining temperature at 70°C (155°F), until chicken is just cooked. Set chicken aside and strain jus in bag. Season jus with salt and pepper to taste. Slice chicken just before serving.

Place cherry tomatoes on a baking tray. Drizzle with olive oil and sprinkle garlic and thyme over.

Preheat oven to 100°C (210°F) and bake tomatoes for 15–17 minutes. Remove from oven and set aside.

Prepare asparagus (see Kitchen Techniques). Bring water to a rapid boil. Use only the top 12 cm (5 in) of 4 asparagus spears, peel and boil for about 4 minutes. Drain and refresh in ice water. Set aside.

Use a vegetable peeler to slice remaining 2 asparagus spears into long strips. Leave raw and set aside.

Prepare artichokes (see Kitchen Techniques). Clean, peel and immediately soak artichokes in ice water mixed with lemon juice and 1 tsp salt to prevent discolouration. Remove from water and slice artichokes and sauté in olive oil until lightly coloured. Sprinkle remaining salt and pepper over.

Serve sliced chicken with cherry tomatoes, boiled and raw asparagus and artichokes, drizzled with chicken jus. Garnish with olives and thyme.

## Togarashi Grilled Squid on Pumpkin Cashew Nut Salad

Preparation Time: 30 minutes   Cooking Time: 40 minutes   Serves 4

### SQUID AND SALAD

Squid *325 g (11¹/2 oz)*

*Shichimi togarashi* (see Note on pg 17) *2 tsp*

Sea salt *¹/4 tsp*

Cashew nuts *55 g (2 oz)*

Vegetable stock (see pg 170) *250 ml (8 fl oz / 1 cup)*

Pumpkin *85 g (3 oz), peeled, seeded and cut into 1-cm (¹/2-in) cubes*

Chopped coriander leaves (cilantro) *¹/2 Tbsp*

### SAUCE

Orange juice *180 ml (6 fl oz / ³/4 cup)*

Shallots *3–4, peeled and sliced*

Garlic *1 clove, peeled and sliced*

Kaffir lime leaf (see Glossary) *1*

Pink peppercorns *1 tsp, lightly crushed*

Olive oil *3 Tbsp*

Chopped parsley leaves *1 tsp*

Wash squid. Remove head and tentacles. Peel off skin. Cut squid into smaller pieces and dry well on absorbent paper.

Score outside surface of squid and marinate with *shichimi togarashi* and sea salt for 10 minutes. Chargrill squid for about 2 minutes on each side until lightly browned and cooked. Alternatively, pan-fry without oil over high heat for 1 minute on each side.

Roast cashew nuts for 20 minutes in a preheated oven at 150°C (300°F). Set aside.

Bring vegetable stock to a boil. Lower pumpkin cubes in to cook for 2–3 minutes until tender but still retaining their shape. Drain and toss with roasted cashew nuts and chopped coriander leaves. Set aside.

Prepare sauce by reducing orange juice by half over medium heat. Add shallots, garlic, lime leaf and pink peppercorns and simmer for 5 minutes. Leave to cool before beating in olive oil. Sprinkle chopped parsley over.

Pour sauce over pumpkin, cashew nuts and squid. Serve.

## Lemon-Marinated Yellow Tail Slices with Artichoke and Rocket Leaves

Start preparations 1 day ahead   Cooking Time: 5 minutes   Serves 4

Dijon mustard $^1/_2$ tsp

Balsamic vinegar *3 Tbsp*

Extra virgin olive oil *85 ml (2$^1/_2$ fl oz / $^1/_3$ cup)*

Olive oil *90 ml (3 fl oz / 6 Tbsp)*

Garlic *1 clove, peeled and finely chopped*

Basil, thyme and rosemary leaves mixture
   *10 g ($^1/_3$ oz) in total*

Fine salt $^1/_4$ tsp

Ground black pepper $^1/_4$ tsp

Yellow tail or barramundi fillet *300 g
   (10$^1/_2$ oz), skinned*

Fine salt $^1/_2$ tsp

Freshly ground black pepper $^1/_2$ tsp

Lemon juice *from 1 lemon*

Artichoke bottoms *100 g (3$^1/_2$ oz), sliced*

Extra virgin olive oil *2 tsp*

Rocket (arugula) leaves *45 g (1$^1/_2$ oz)*

Cherry tomatoes *85 g (3 oz), each cut in half*

Pine nuts *10 g ($^1/_3$ oz), toasted until
   lightly browned*

Combine ingredients for vinaigrette and mix well. Leave to stand refrigerated for 24 hours. Strain before using.

Slice fish fillet very thinly to obtain 16 slices. Season with salt, pepper and lemon juice. Leave to marinate for 2 minutes.

Prepare artichoke bottoms (see Kitchen Techniques). Sauté artichokes quickly in extra virgin olive oil.

Toss marinated fish, artichokes, rocket leaves and cherry tomatoes with vinaigrette. Sprinkle with toasted pine nuts and serve.

## Corn Nut-Crusted Short Ribs

Start preparations 1 day ahead   Cooking Time: 7 hours   Serves 4

### RED WINE MARINADE

Red wine (Burgundy or Bordeaux) *300 ml (10 fl oz / 1¼ cups)*

White onions *110 g (4 oz), peeled and thinly sliced*

Garlic *1 head, cut horizontally in half*

Carrots *55 g (2 oz), peeled and thinly sliced*

Celery *55 g (2 oz), finely chopped*

Sage *2 sprigs*

Rosemary *2 sprigs*

Flat-leaf (Italian) parsley (see Glossary) *2 sprigs*

Bay leaves *2*

Thyme *2 sprigs*

Fine salt *¼ tsp*

Ground black pepper *¼ tsp*

### SHORT RIBS

Dakota bison short ribs or beef short ribs *1 kg (2 lb 3 oz), silver skin removed*

Plain (all-purpose) flour *110 g (4 oz)*

Fine salt *¼ tsp*

Ground black pepper *⅛ tsp*

Grape seed oil *125 ml (4 fl oz / ½ cup)*

Corn nuts *30 g (1 oz), ground*

### CORN GRITS

Grits *110 g (4 oz)*

Water *1 litre (32 fl oz/ 4 cups)*

Fine salt *½–1 tsp*

Ground black pepper *½ tsp*

### CORN PURÉE

Summer corn *2 ears, kernels cut*

Water *235 ml (7½ fl oz), mixed with ⅛ tsp salt*

Ground black pepper *⅛ tsp*

### RAINBOW SWISS CHARD

Water *1 litre (32 fl oz / 4 cups), mixed with ⅛ tsp salt*

Rainbow Swiss chard *225 g (8 oz)*

Fine salt *⅛ tsp*

Ground black pepper *⅛ tsp*

**NOTE**

Corn nuts are a favourite snack of baseball fans in the US. To prepare corn nuts, dried corn kernels are first soaked in water for 2–3 days in the refrigerator. The softened corn kernels are then drained and dried before being deep-fried and salted.

Grits are coarsely ground dried corn kernels from which the hull and germ have been removed. Grits are usually cooked with milk or water and eaten as a cereal or side dish.

Blanching is a method of quick cooking where ingredients are plunged into boiling liquid, usually water, but sometimes also oil. This quickly seals the surfaces of the ingredient, locking in moisture. The blanched ingredient is then drained and, in the case of vegetables, placed into a bowl of ice water to stop the cooking process.

Prepare red wine marinade. Combine all ingredients in a small stockpot and bring to a boil. Let mixture cook for 20 minutes and taste to ensure alcohol has evaporated. Remove from heat and cool in an ice bath.

Prepare short ribs. Lay short ribs in a single layer in a roasting pan and pour red wine marinade over. Cover with plastic wrap (cling film) and let sit overnight. Remove ribs from marinade and strain marinade. Reserve residue of vegetables.

Combine flour, salt and pepper. Dust ribs and shake off any excess flour. Heat oil over medium-high heat, then sear ribs on all sides over high heat until golden brown.

Place seared ribs in a roasting pan and add strained marinade and vegetables. Bring marinade to a boil then remove roasting pan from heat and cover with aluminium foil. Place in a preheated oven at 150°C (300°F) for 4–6 hours, or until meat begins to fall off bones. Remove foil and leave ribs to sit in juices overnight.

Remove ribs from roasting pan and cut the meat into 3.5-cm (1½-in) cubes, trimming off any remaining fat. Bring any remaining marinade to a gentle simmer and reheat ribs just before crusting with ground corn nuts.

Prepare corn grits. Using a double boiler, add grits to water and cook over low heat for 3–4 hours, stirring occasionally, until grits are tender but still have some crunch. Remove from heat and season with salt and pepper. Keep warm.

Prepare corn purée. In a saucepan, bring corn kernels and water to a simmer and cook for 5–6 minutes. Remove from heat and purée until smooth. Season with pepper and keep warm.

Prepare chard just before serving. Bring water to a boil. Peel leaves from chard, tear into bite-size pieces and blanch. Dice stems and blanch. Season leaves and stems with salt and pepper.

Serve ribs with corn grits, corn purée and chard. Garnish as desired.

# Soups

A bowl of piping hot soup at the end of a cold winter's day is sublimely comforting, imparting a deep warmth to the body and the spirit. On a hot summer afternoon, a cold soup imbibed with nature's goodness immediately refreshes and invigorates. Mothers all over the world are known to brew a good bowl of soup to nurse their children's colds and uplift their spirits. The soups presented in the following pages reflect that tenderness and thought in their ingredients and preparation ideas. Shellfish, Mullet, Black Cod and Papaya Bisque with Garlic Focaccia nourishes the body and improves digestion, Minted Pea Soup offers a refreshing twist on the traditional pea soup with its use of fresh mint leaves, while the other *Naturally Peninsula* soup selections will surely impress you with their appetising flavours coupled with a healthy serving of vitamins and antioxidant nutrients!

## Minted Pea Soup

Preparation Time: 30 minutes   Cooking Time: 1 hour   Serves 4

### PEA BROTH

**English peas** *700 g (1¹/₂ lb)*

**Leeks** *125 g (4¹/₂ oz), cut into 2-cm (1-in) cubes*

**White wine** *125 ml (4 fl oz / ¹/₂ cup)*

**Bay leaf** *1*

**Garlic** *1 clove*

**Water** *2 litres (64 fl oz / 8 cups)*

### FOR PEA SOUP

**Mint leaves** *12*

**Lemon juice** *60 ml (2 fl oz / 4 Tbsp)*

**Fine salt** *¹/₄ tsp or to taste*

**Ground black pepper** *¹/₄ tsp*

### GARNISH

**Greek yoghurt** *60 ml (2 fl oz / 4 Tbsp)*

**Water** *2 Tbsp*

Prepare pea broth. Shell peas and set peas aside for use in pea soup. Rinse pea pods (shells) and place into a large pot with leeks, white wine, bay leaf and garlic. Cover with water and bring to a boil. When water comes to a boil, reduce to low heat and simmer for 1 hour. Strain and discard leeks, bay leaf, pea pods and garlic. Leave broth to cool before refrigerating to chill.

Prepare pea soup. Bring a pot of lightly salted water to a boil and blanch (see Note on pg 31) shelled peas for about 30 seconds. Drain and cool peas immediately in an ice bath. Reserve some peas and blend remaining peas with 625 ml (20 fl oz / 2¹/₂ cups) chilled pea broth, mint leaves and lemon juice in a blender (food processor) for 3–4 minutes. Strain purée through a fine mesh sieve and season with salt and pepper.

Place reserved peas into glasses. Blend (process) yoghurt with water and pour over peas. Top with pea soup and serve.

## Shellfish, Mullet, Black Cod and Papaya Bisque with Garlic Focaccia

Preparation Time: 30 minutes   Cooking Time: 2 hours   Serves 4

Golden mullet tails *4*

Ripe papaya *1, about 300 g (10¹/2 oz), peeled and seeded*

Olive oil *2 Tbsp*

Black cod fillet *100 g (3¹/2 oz), skinned and cut into 1-cm (¹/2-in) dice*

Mussels *280 g (10 oz), cleaned and debearded*

Shallots *20 g (²/3 oz), peeled and chopped*

Dry white wine *125 ml (4 fl oz / ¹/2 cup)*

Noilly Prat *125 ml (4 fl oz / ¹/2 cup)*

Chicken stock (see pg 171) *2 litres (64 fl oz / 8 cups)*

Fine salt *¹/2 tsp*

Ground black pepper *¹/4 tsp*

GARNISH

Garlic focaccia toasts* *4 slices, or croutons of choice*

**NOTE**

Noilly Prat is a dry, fortified wine flavoured with aromatic herbs and spices. Using an open-air ageing process, the wines are first matured in large oak casks for 8 months inside storehouses. Contact with the oak strengthens the body of the wine. The wines are then transferred to different oak barrels and left in the open-air for a year. The result is a unique fortified wine.

Trim and debone mullet tails but keep tail fin for presentation. Slice mullet into 5-cm (2-in) pieces.

Cut three-quarters of papaya into 1-cm (¹/2-in) dice. Cut remaining papaya into 4 even pieces.

Heat olive oil in a saucepan with a lid and sauté diced papaya, cod, mussels and shallots for about 30 seconds. Add remaining papaya. Add white wine and Noilly Prat and increase to high heat. Cover and cook for 10 seconds, or until mussels open up. Once this happens, remove mussels and 4 pieces of papaya. Set aside.

Reduce stock to one-third and add chicken stock. Cook over medium heat and allow liquid to reduce to half. Adjust seasoning with salt and pepper.

Meanwhile, prepare 4 soup bowls and place a piece of papaya into each bowl.

Steam mullet pieces and tail fins for about 4 minutes and place into soup bowls on top of papaya.

Reheat mussels by plunging into stock for 30 seconds. Ladle hot stock and mussels over mullet.

Garnish each bowl of soup with garlic focaccia toast. If desired, use a melon baller on extra papaya flesh to obtain added garnishing. Serve immediately.

## *Garlic Focaccia Toast

Butter *30 g (1 oz), softened at room temperature*

Garlic *6 cloves, peeled and finely chopped*

Thyme *6 sprigs, stalks removed and leaves finely chopped*

Fine salt *¹/4 tsp*

Focaccia bread *4 thin slices*

Combine butter, garlic, thyme and salt. Spread a thin layer on one side of focaccia bread.

Toast under a grill or in a hot toaster oven for 30 seconds until butter melts and bread is lightly crisp.

## Tomato Consommé with Mushroom Wonton, Sago Pearls and Tofu

Preparation Time: 3 hours   Cooking Time: 45 minutes   Serves 4

### TOMATO CONSOMMÉ

Very ripe plum (Roma) tomatoes *2 kg*
   *(4 lb 6 oz)*

Fine salt *¹/₂ tsp*

Ground black pepper *¹/₄ tsp*

### MUSHROOM WONTONS

Olive oil *2 tsp*

Shallots *30 g (1 oz), peeled and finely sliced*

Fresh seasonal mushrooms *85 g (3 oz), sliced*

Fine salt *¹/₂ tsp*

Ground black pepper *¹/₄ tsp*

Basil leaves *7, chopped*

Chopped parsley *1 Tbsp*

Wonton wrappers *4 sheets, each 7-cm
   (3-in) square*

Water *1 Tbsp*

Canola oil *500 ml (16 fl oz / 2 cups)*

### GARNISH

Sago pearls *45 g (1¹/₂ oz)*

Tofu *55 g (2 oz), cut into 3-cm (1¹/₂-in) squares*

Tomatoes *55 g (2 oz), peeled, seeded and cut
   into wedges*

Coriander leaves (cilantro) *12*

**NOTE**
Sago pearls are processed from the starch of the sago palm. Sago pearls can be used in both sweet and savoury preparations and as a thickener in desserts.

To peel a tomato, use a sharp knife to mark an 'X' on the skin of the tomato. Quickly blanch in boiling water for 20 seconds. Drain and refresh in ice water immediately. The skin can then be easily peeled off using the tip of a sharp knife.

Prepare tomato consommé. Core tomatoes and chop coarsely using a blender (food processor). Transfer to a stockpot and bring to a rapid boil over medium-high heat for 5 minutes. Pour tomatoes into a muslin cloth strainer and let tomato essence drip into a bowl. This will take 2–3 hours. There will be about 1 litre (32 fl oz / 4 cups) of essence. Return tomato essence to stockpot and reduce to half over medium heat. Takes about 30 minutes. Strain and season with salt and pepper. Set aside.

Prepare mushroom wontons. Heat olive oil and sauté shallots and mushrooms over high heat for 2 minutes. Season with salt and pepper. Add basil and parsley. Reserve a quarter of mushrooms for soup garnish. Set aside and keep warm.

Place a spoonful of sautéed mushrooms in the centre of each wonton wrapper. Brush edges of wonton wrappers lightly with water and bring edges up to enclose filling.

Heat canola oil and deep-fry wontons for 2 minutes or until golden brown and crisp. Set aside to drain on absorbent paper.

Bring a pot of water to a boil and cook sago pearls for 3 minutes or until pearls are translucent. Drain well.

Place sago pearls, tofu squares, tomatoes and reserved sautéed mushrooms in soup plates. Ladle consommé over and arrange wonton on top. Garnish with coriander leaves.

## Watermelon and Cherry Tomato Soup

Preparation Time: 40 minutes   Cooking Time: Nil   Serves 4

**Watermelon flesh** *450 g (1 lb), seeded and chopped*

**Garlic** *3 cloves, peeled*

**Cherry tomatoes** *280 g (10 oz)*

**Cranberry juice** *180 ml (6 fl oz / ³/₄ cup)*

**Lime juice** *2 Tbsp*

**Cayenne pepper** *1 tsp*

**Fine salt** *¹/₂ tsp*

**Ground black pepper** *¹/₄ tsp*

**Plum (Roma) tomatoes** *2, peeled (see Note on pg 39), seeded and diced*

**Yam bean (jicama)** *140 g (5 oz), peeled and diced*

**English cucumbers** *140 g (5 oz), cored, seeded and diced*

**Mint leaves** *a handful*

**Black peppercorns** *¹/₄ tsp, roughly ground*

**NOTE**

Yam bean (jicama) is a tan-skinned tuber with a mild, sweetish flavour and crisp, crunchy texture. The skin is not edible and should be peeled before using. Yam bean can be eaten raw or cooked.

English or hothouse cucumbers are almost seedless, uniformly shaped and less bitter than other varieties. They have a crisp flesh and are said to be more easily digestible, as the seeds are smaller.

Place watermelon, garlic, cherry tomatoes, cranberry juice and lime juice in a blender (food processor) and purée until fine.

Season with cayenne pepper, salt and pepper. Refrigerate to chill soup.

Divide plum tomatoes, yam bean and cucumbers among 4 soup bowls. Top with chilled soup and garnish with mint leaves. Sprinkle with black pepper. If desired, use a melon baller on extra watermelon flesh to obtain added garnishing. Serve immediately.

## Butternut and Pumpkin Soup

Preparation Time: 20 minutes   Cooking Time: 1 hour 45 minutes   Serves 4

**Butternut pumpkin** *700 g (1¹/₂ lb), peeled and cut into 2-cm (1-in) cubes*

**Pumpkin** *450 g (16 oz), peeled and cut into 2-cm (1-in) cubes*

**Ground allspice** *¹/₂ Tbsp*

**Ground cinnamon** *¹/₂ Tbsp*

**Ground cloves** *1 tsp*

**Olive oil** *1 Tbsp*

**Butter** *30 g (1 oz)*

**Onions** *125 g (4¹/₂ oz), peeled and cut into 2-cm (1-in) cubes*

**Leeks** *125 g (4¹/₂ oz), peeled and cut into 2-cm (1-in) cubes*

**Fennel bulb (see Glossary)** *125 g (4¹/₂ oz), peeled and cut into 2-cm (1-in) cubes*

**Vegetable stock (see pg 170)** *1.5 litres (48 fl oz / 6 cups)*

**Fine salt** *³/₄ tsp or to taste*

**Ground black pepper** *¹/₄ tsp or to taste*

GARNISH

**Olive oil** *¹/₂ Tbsp*

**Dried apple** *30 g (1 oz), cut into 2-cm (1-in) cubes*

**Oregano leaves**

Dust butternut pumpkin and pumpkin cubes liberally with ground allspice, cinnamon and cloves. Sprinkle olive oil over and slow roast in a preheated oven at 180°C (350°F) for 1 hour.

Heat butter and sweat (see Note on pg 20) onions, leeks and fennel over medium-low heat until soft.

Add roasted butternut pumpkin and pumpkin and vegetable stock and bring to a boil. Simmer over low heat for 30 minutes, then purée in a blender (food processor). Strain purée and discard residue. Season to taste with salt and pepper. Pour soup into soup bowls.

Prepare garnish. Heat olive oil and sauté dried apple over medium-high heat until golden brown.

Garnish soup with sautéed dried apple and oregano leaves. Serve hot.

# Fish

Seared, poached, baked, steamed, pan-fried — *Naturally Peninsula* fish comes in a variety of interesting guises, from the lively flavours of the Hawaiian Onaga Kama with Truffle-Yaki Sauce, Sake-Braised Vegetables, Wasabi Oil and Lotus Root Chips, to the tender and succulent Confit Salmon with Couscous and Tomato Vierge Sauce. You will be amazed at the exciting fish creations from the chefs of The Peninsula Hotels, each offering a unique and tantalising culinary experience. Whether it's the Spring Herb Onaga with Preserved Lemon Quinoa and Heirloom Tomato Salad, or the Tai Snapper with Forbidden Rice, Baby Choy Sum and Tamarind Banana Curry, innovative cooking methods are paired with cleverly juxtaposed flavours and textures to seduce your taste buds time and again.

# Confit Salmon with Couscous and Tomato Vierge Sauce

Preparation Time: 1 hour   Cooking Time: 40 minutes   Serves 4

### SALMON CONFIT

Salmon fillet *500 g (1 lb 1¹/₂ oz), skinned and cleaned*

Parchment paper *15-cm (6-in) square*

Olive oil *1 litre (32 fl oz / 4 cups)*

### SALMON MARINADE

Kosher or rough salt *5 tsp*

Sugar *5 tsp*

White peppercorns *¹/₂ tsp, crushed*

Chopped dill *1 Tbsp*

Finely grated lemon zest *2 tsp*

### COUSCOUS

Water *100 ml (3¹/₂ fl oz / ³/₈ cup)*

Salt *¹/₂ tsp*

Olive oil *2 tsp*

Couscous (see Glossary) *100 g (3¹/₂ oz)*

Pumpkin seeds *30 g (1 oz), toasted*

Pine nuts *30 g (1 oz), toasted*

Flat-leaf (Italian) parsley (see Glossary) *10 g (¹/₃ oz), finely sliced*

Basil leaves *15 g (¹/₂ oz), finely sliced*

Olive oil *2 Tbsp*

Lemon juice *1 Tbsp*

Cayenne pepper *¹/₄ tsp*

Salt *¹/₄ tsp*

Ground black pepper *¹/₈ tsp*

### TOMATO VIERGE

Extra virgin olive oil *200 ml (6 fl oz / ³/₄ cup)*

Lemon juice *1 tsp*

Tomatoes *100 g (3¹/₂ oz), peeled (see Note on pg 39), seeded and diced*

English peas *70 g (2¹/₂ oz)*

Basil leaves *20 g (²/₃ oz), finely sliced*

Salt *¹/₂ tsp*

Sugar *2 tsp*

Ground black pepper *¹/₂ tsp*

### GARNISH

Mesclun or salad leaves of choice *60 g (2 oz)*

Combine ingredients for salmon marinade in a bowl. Place salmon in to marinate for 20 minutes. Remove salmon from marinade and quickly rinse in cold water. Pat dry and divide into 4 equal portions.

Prepare salmon confit (see Note on pg 24). Line base of a medium-sized saucepan with parchment paper and add olive oil. Heat to 50°C (120°F). Use a cooking thermometer to measure the temperature. Place salmon in oil and cook slowly, maintaining a constant temperature for 40 minutes. Leave thermometer in oil to monitor temperature, but do not let it touch the bottom of pan.

Remove and place salmon on absorbent paper to absorb excess oil. Keep salmon warm in a lightly heated oven or under a slow grill while preparing rest of dish.

Prepare couscous. Bring water, salt and olive oil to a boil. Add couscous and mix well. Cover with plastic wrap (cling film) and remove from heat. Leave to stand for about 4 minutes until grains swell and liquid is absorbed. Mix in remaining ingredients and season with salt and pepper. Keep at room temperature. Just prior to serving, taste and adjust seasoning as couscous can become bland when grains swell.

Prepare tomato vierge. Warm olive oil lightly and add remaining ingredients. Taste for seasoning and keep at room temperature.

To serve, spoon couscous onto serving plates. Drain most of the oil away from tomato vierge and arrange on serving plates. Top with salmon and garnish with salad leaves.

## Steamed Sea Bass with Shallots and Green Peppercorns (Pla Nueng Sa-Moon-Prai)

Preparation Time: 30 minutes   Cooking Time: 10 minutes   Serves 4

Vegetable stock (see pg 170) *3 Tbsp*

Lemon grass (see Glossary) *45 g (1¹/₂ oz), ends trimmed, hard outer leaves removed, use only bulbous end, chopped*

Shallots *85 g (3 oz), peeled*

Garlic *85 g (3 oz), peeled*

Fresh Thai green peppercorns *20*

Sea bass fillets *4, each about 200 g (7 oz), with skin*

Red Thai bird's eye chillies (see Glossary) *5, chopped*

Coriander leaves (cilantro) *10 g (¹/₃ oz)*

Light soy sauce *90 ml (3 fl oz / 6 Tbsp)*

Bok choy or other greens *200 g (7 oz), steamed or blanched*

GARNISH

Red chilli *1, seeded and cut into fine julienne*

Crisp-fried shallots

Crisp-fried garlic

Coriander leaves (cilantro)

Lime *1, cut into wedges*

Blend (process) vegetable stock, lemon grass, shallots, garlic and green peppercorns together to obtain a purée.

Place fillets into purée and leave to marinate for 10 minutes. Remove fillets from marinade and place on a steaming plate. Top with bird's eye chillies and coriander leaves and drizzle with light soy sauce. Spoon 2 Tbsp marinade over.

Steam marinated fillets for 4–6 minutes over high heat until flesh turns opaque white and a skewer can be easily inserted into the thickest part of fish.

Serve fish with bok choy or other greens. Garnish with chilli, crisp-fried shallots, garlic, coriander leaves and lime wedges.

## Alaskan Black Cod with Lemon-Scented Fingerling Potatoes, Cauliflower and Chervil Pesto

Preparation Time: 45 minutes   Cooking Time: 40 minutes   Serves 4

CHERVIL PESTO

Chervil *60 g (2 oz)*

Parsley *30 g (1 oz)*

Tarragon *15 g ($^1$/$_2$ oz)*

Pine nuts *15 g ($^1$/$_2$ oz)*

Garlic *1 clove, peeled*

Shallot *1, peeled*

Lemon juice *2 Tbsp*

Olive oil *45 ml (1 $^1$/$_2$ fl oz / 3 Tbsp)*

LEMON POTATOES

Fingerling or russet potatoes *800 g (1$^3$/$_4$ lb), cleaned and peeled*

Cold water *2 litres (64 fl oz / 8 cups)*

Extra virgin olive oil *2 Tbsp*

Lemon juice *1 tsp*

Fine salt *1 tsp*

Ground white pepper *$^1$/$_4$ tsp*

COD

Cooking oil *1 Tbsp*

Alaskan black cod *4 pieces, each about 180 g (6$^1$/$_2$ oz)*

Fine salt *$^1$/$_2$ tsp*

Ground black pepper *$^1$/$_2$ tsp*

VEGETABLES

Baby cauliflower (white, orange and/or purple if available) *200 g (7 oz), cut into bite-size florets*

Baby Romanesco *100 g (3$^1$/$_2$ oz), cut into bite-size florets*

Water *1 litre (32 fl oz / 4 cups), mixed with 1 tsp salt*

Fine salt *$^1$/$_4$ tsp*

Ground black pepper *$^1$/$_8$ tsp*

**NOTE**
Romanesco is a vegetable hailing from Italy that resembles cauliflower. The plant forms a head of pointed florets which have a pale lime green hue and an unusual mosiac pattern. It has a taste and texture exceeding the finest cauliflower.

Prepare chervil pesto. Blanch (see Note on pg 31) herbs in a large pot of lightly salted boiling water for about 30 seconds, then submerge in ice cold water. Remove and drain.

Squeeze out all excess water from herbs, then place in a blender (processor) with pine nuts, garlic and shallot. Add lemon juice and blend until smooth. Add oil in small amounts and continue blending until a smooth homogenous mixture is achieved.

Prepare potatoes. Put potatoes in a pot and cover with cold water. Bring to a boil, then reduce to a simmer. Cook until potatoes are tender. Takes 20–25 minutes. Drain potatoes, then mash with olive oil and lemon juice using a potato masher. Season with salt and pepper. Store in a warm place until ready to use.

Prepare cod. Heat oil in a non-stick pan over medium-high heat. Season cod with salt and pepper and place skin-side down in pan. Cook for 2 minutes, then bake in a 190°C (370°F) oven for 4–5 minutes.

Prepare vegetables. Blanch vegetables in a pot of lightly salted boiling water for about 30 seconds. Drain well and season with salt and pepper.

Serve cod with mashed potatoes and vegetables. Drizzle with chervil pesto. Garnish as desired.

## Spring Herb Onaga with Preserved Lemon Quinoa and Heirloom Tomato Salad

Preparation Time: 2 hours   Cooking Time: 40 minutes   Serves 4

Onaga or red snapper fillets *4, each about 240 g (9 oz), boneless*

Fine salt *¹/₂ tsp*

Ground black pepper *¹/₄ tsp*

Olive oil *45 ml (1¹/₂ fl oz / 3 Tbsp)*

### MIXED FRESH HERBS

Thyme *5 sprigs, stalks discarded*

Parsley leaves *2 Tbsp*

Chervil leaves *2 Tbsp*

Tarragon leaves *2 Tbsp*

Chives *2 Tbsp*

### LEMON QUINOA

Olive oil *¹/₂ Tbsp*

Shallots *2, peeled and chopped*

Preserved lemon *1, cut in half*

Quinoa (see Glossary) *55 g (2 oz), rinsed in cold water and drained*

Vegetable stock (see pg 170) *250 ml (8 fl oz / 1 cup)*

Saffron threads *¹/₈ tsp*

Lemon juice *1 tsp*

Fine salt *¹/₄ tsp*

Ground black pepper *¹/₈ tsp*

### HERB VINAIGRETTE

Champagne vinegar *1 Tbsp*

Extra virgin olive oil *125 ml (2 fl oz / ¹/₂ cup)*

Shallots *15 g (¹/₂ oz), peeled and chopped*

Mixed herbs *15 g (¹/₂ oz)*

Fine salt *¹/₄ tsp*

Ground black pepper *¹/₄ tsp*

### TOMATO SALAD

Assorted heirloom tomatoes or plum (Roma) tomatoes *450 g (16 oz), cut into small wedges and seeded*

Watermelon radish or radish *100 g (3¹/₃ oz), peeled and diced*

Fine salt *¹/₄ tsp*

Coarsely ground black pepper *¹/₈ tsp*

### ROCKET PESTO

Pine nuts *30 g (1 oz), toasted*

Garlic *2 cloves, peeled*

Basil leaves *10*

Rocket (arugula) leaves *220 g (8 oz)*

Extra virgin olive oil *125 ml (4 fl oz / ¹/₂ cup)*

Salt *¹/₄ tsp*

Ground black pepper *¹/₄ tsp*

### RED CAPSICUM VINAIGRETTE

Large red capsicums (bell peppers) *240 g (8¹/₂ oz), cored, seeded and roughly chopped*

Water *2 Tbsp*

Champagne vinegar *1 tsp*

Fine salt *¹/₈ tsp*

Ground black pepper *¹/₈ tsp*

Olive oil *1 Tbsp*

**NOTE**

Watermelon radish is a round root vegetable with a green rind and red flesh which resembles that of a watermelon. Add a splash of vinegar and the red colour becomes more intense. Watermelon radish can be eaten raw or cooked.

Onaga is a Hawaiian fish better known by its Japanese name than its Hawaiian name, Ula`ula. It is also called ruby snapper or longtail snapper. Onaga kama refers to the collar of the fish.

Heirloom tomatoes are open-pollinated tomatoes (as opposed to commercially grown hybrid tomatoes) which come in an amazing range of colours, shapes, tastes and textures.

To make preserved lemons, scrub 5 lemons, dry well and cut into wedges. Toss with 150 g (5¹/₃ oz / ³/₄ cup) coarse salt and put into a glass jar with 250 ml (8 fl oz / 1 cup) lemon juice, 1 bay leaf and 2 cloves. Cover with a tight-fitting lid and leave in a cool place for 1 week, giving the jar a good shake once a day. When ready, add olive oil to cover the lemons, replace the lid and store refrigerated.

Prepare mixed herbs. Combine herbs and chop. Mix well.

Prepare fillets. Sprinkle fillets with salt and pepper, then coat one side of each fillet with mixed herbs.

Heat a non-stick pan over high heat and add olive oil. Place fillets into pan, herb-side down. Pan-fry for 3 minutes until brown, then flip fillets over and cook until just opaque in the middle. Set aside.

Prepare lemon quinoa. In a small saucepan, heat olive oil and sauté shallots over medium-high heat for 2 minutes. Add preserved lemon, quinoa, vegetable stock and saffron. Cover and cook for 15 minutes over medium heat. When done, quinoa should be tender and the germ visible. Remove lemon and season with lemon juice, salt and pepper. Set aside and keep warm.

Prepare herb vinaigrette. Whisk champagne vinegar, olive oil, shallots and mixed herbs together in a small bowl. Season with salt and pepper. Set aside.

Prepare tomato salad. Combine tomatoes and watermelon radish or radish. Toss with herb vinaigrette and sprinkle with salt and pepper.

Prepare rocket pesto. Place toasted pine nuts, garlic, basil, rocket and olive oil into a blender (food processor) and blend at medium speed to achieve a purée. Season with salt and pepper and refrigerate until needed.

Prepare red capsicum vinaigrette. Place chopped capsicums into a blender (food processor) with water and blend until a purée is achieved. Place into a small saucepan and cook for 3 minutes. Strain juice through a fine mesh sieve and return to saucepan. Cook, stirring, until reduced to 2 Tbsp. Pour vinaigrette into a small bowl and stir in remaining ingredients. Set aside until needed.

Serve fillets with quinoa and tomato salad. Drizzle with rocket pesto and red capsicum vinaigrette. Garnish as desired.

## Pan-Seared Arctic Char with Sweet Potato, Saffron Nage and Tempura Long Bean

Preparation Time: 30 minutes   Cooking Time: 1 hour   Serves 4

Arctic char, salmon or trout fillet *680 g (24 oz), with skin, cut into 4 pieces*

Olive oil *2 Tbsp*

### NAGE

Vegetable oil *1 Tbsp*

White fish bones *900 g (32 oz)*

Onion *55 g (2 oz), peeled and cut into cubes*

Celery *55 g (2 oz), trimmed and cut into cubes*

Garlic *1 head, cut horizontally in half*

Fennel bulb (see Glossary) *55 g (2 oz), cut into cubes*

Dry white wine *250 ml (8 fl oz / 1 cup)*

Water *2 litres (64 fl oz / 8 cups)*

Saffron threads *1/8–1/4 tsp*

Lemon *1, squeezed for juice, zest and pulp reserved*

Vanilla bean *1 pod, split open*

Bay leaves *3*

Fine salt *1/4 tsp*

Ground white pepper *1/4 tsp*

### VEGETABLES

Spinach leaves *450 g (16 oz), washed and drained*

Fine salt *1/8 tsp*

Ground black pepper *1/8 tsp*

Sweet potatoes *240 g (8 oz), peeled and cut into 1-cm (1/2-in) cubes*

Water *1 litre (32 fl oz / 4 cups), mixed with 2 tsp salt*

### TEMPURA LONG BEAN

Tempura flour *100 g (31/2 oz)*

Long bean *1, trimmed and cut into length of fish pieces*

Canola oil *1 litre (32 fl oz / 4 cups)*

### NOTE

Nage is an aromatic seafood broth flavoured with herbs and vegetables. It is sometimes reduced before being served with the main items of the dish.

Deglazing is a technique used to create a flavourful base for sauces or gravies. The small bits of browned food particles adhering to the pan after sautéing are loosened by adding a small amount of liquid (wine, stock, lemon juice, etc.) to the pan and stirring.

Arctic char is farmed in Iceland. It has pink flesh and a flavour that is a cross between trout and salmon.

Prepare nage before cooking fish. Heat oil and sweat (see Note on pg 20) fish bones, onion, celery, garlic and fennel over medium heat for 15 minutes, ensuring that vegetables do not turn brown. Deglaze with white wine, then add water, saffron, lemon juice, lemon zest and pulp, vanilla bean and bay leaves. Bring to a boil, then reduce to a simmer for 30 minutes. Strain, return to heat and continue cooking to reduce mixture to about 300 ml (10 fl oz / 11/4 cups). Season with salt and pepper.

Meanwhile, score fish fillets. Heat olive oil in a pan and sear fillets, skin side down until skin is crisp. Takes about 3 minutes. Turn fish over and fry other side for another 3 minutes. If fillet is thick, transfer to a 240°C (465°F) oven and bake for 5 minutes until medium-rare. Set aside.

Steam spinach briefly until colour changes. Drain and season with salt and pepper. Keep warm.

Bring a pot of water to a boil and cook sweet potatoes until tender. Drain.

Prepare tempura long beans. Prepare tempura batter according to instructions on pack. Heat oil to 180°C (350°F). Dip long bean lengths in tempura batter and deep-fry until crisp. Drain well.

Serve fish with spinach, sweet potatoes, tempura long bean and nage.

## Pistachio-Crusted Dover Sole with Lemon Grass-Coconut Nage, Bok Choy and Spaetzle

Preparation Time: 1 hour   Cooking Time: 1 hour 20 minutes   Serves 4

### SPAETZLE

Plain (all-purpose) flour *280 g (10 oz)*

Eggs *2*

Milk *125 ml (4 fl oz / 1/2 cup)*

Fine salt *1/3 tsp*

Baking powder *1/4 tsp*

Water *1 litre (32 fl oz / 4 cups), mixed with 1 tsp salt*

Butter *2 Tbsp*

Ground white pepper *1/4 tsp*

### LEMON GRASS-COCONUT NAGE

Olive oil *1 Tbsp*

Garlic *2 cloves, peeled and chopped*

Ginger *30 g (1 oz), peeled and chopped*

Lemon grass *1 stalk, ends trimmed, hard outer leaves removed, use only bulbous end, crushed*

Shallots *30 g (1 oz), peeled and chopped*

Coconut milk *625 ml (20 fl oz / 2 1/2 cups)*

Fish stock (see pg 171) *1 litre (32 fl oz / 4 cups)*

Kaffir lime leaves (see Glossary) *10, crushed*

Dover sole fillets *4, each about 175 g (6 1/2 oz)*

Fine salt *2/3 tsp*

Ground black pepper *1/3 tsp*

### FOR DOVER SOLE FILLET

Fine salt *1/8 tsp*

Ground black pepper *1/8 tsp*

Honey mustard *125 ml (4 fl oz / 1/2 cup)*

Pistachio nuts *70 g (2 1/2 oz), ground*

### BOK CHOY

Water *1 litre (32 fl oz / 4 cups), mixed with 1 tsp salt*

Baby bok choy *4 stalks, each about 45g (1 1/2 oz), cut in half*

Fine salt *1/8 tsp*

Ground black pepper *1/8 tsp*

### NOTE

Spaetzle is a German dish of mini noodles or dumplings made with flour, eggs, water and/or milk, salt and sometimes nutmeg. The dough is often boiled before being sautéed with butter and served as a side dish or added to soups and other dishes.

Gratinate means to cook food that has first been covered with buttered crumbs, shredded cheese or chopped nuts under a hot grill until a crisp crust forms.

Prepare spaetzle. Combine flour, eggs, milk, 1/8 tsp salt and baking powder into a paste and mix well. Bring salted water to a boil and lower heat to simmer. Force paste through a potato ricer or sieve into simmering water. Cook until spaetzle rises to the surface. Remove with a slotted spoon and set aside to cool. Just before serving, melt butter in a saucepan. Add spaetzle and sauté briefly over high heat. Season with pepper and remaining salt and serve immediately.

Prepare lemon grass-coconut nage (see Note on page 54). Heat oil and sweat (see Note on pg 20) garlic, ginger, lemon grass and shallots over medium-high heat for 2 minutes. Add coconut milk and fish stock. Bring to a boil and add kaffir lime leaves. Reduce heat and simmer for 20 minutes. Add fillets and poach (see Note on pg 24) for 3 minutes. Remove and set aside. Reduce stock over low heat for 15–20 minutes. Season to taste with 1/2 tsp salt and 1/4 tsp pepper. Keep warm.

Sprinkle remaining salt and pepper over fillets. Coat with honey mustard and sprinkle ground pistachio nuts over. Gratinate under a grill or in an oven until brown.

Blanch (see Note on pg 31) bok choy in lightly salted boiling water. Drain and season to taste with salt and pepper.

Serve fillets with hot spaetzle, bok choy and nage. Garnish as desired.

## Tai Snapper with Forbidden Rice, Baby Choy Sum and Tamarind Banana Curry

Preparation Time: 30 minutes   Cooking Time: 1 hour   Serves 4

### TAI SNAPPER

Tai snapper fillets 4, *each about 150 g (5¹/₃ oz), cut in half*

Fine salt ¹/₂ *tsp*

Ground black pepper ¹/₄ *tsp*

Olive oil 1 *Tbsp*

### FORBIDDEN RICE

Forbidden rice 195 g (7 oz), *washed and drained*

Water 360 ml (12 fl oz / 1¹/₂ cups)

Chicken stock (see pg 171) 2 *Tbsp*

### TAMARIND BANANA CURRY

Butter 55 g (2 oz)

Shallots 3, *peeled and chopped*

Ripe bananas 4, *each about 140 g (5 oz), peeled and chopped just before using*

Fish curry powder 3 *Tbsp*

Tamarind pulp 15 g (¹/₂ oz), *weighed without seeds*

Chicken stock (see pg 171) 250 ml (8 fl oz / 1 cup)

Lime juice 60 ml (2 fl oz / ¹/₄ cup)

Coriander leaves (cilantro) 30 g (1 oz), *chopped*

Fine salt ¹/₈ *tsp*

Ground black pepper ¹/₈ *tsp*

### VEGETABLES

Canola oil 1 *Tbsp*

Baby choy sum 4 stalks, *each about 50 g (2 oz)*

Hon shimeiji mushrooms 70 g (2¹/₂ oz), *ends trimmed*

Red capsicums (bell peppers) 120 g (4¹/₂ oz), *cored and seeded, cut into fine julienne*

Fine salt ¹/₄ *tsp*

Ground black pepper ¹/₈ *tsp*

### GARNISH

Lotus root chips (optional) (see pg 61) 8

**NOTE**

Tai snapper is a sea bream, but its similarities to red snapper in terms of appearance and taste are striking.

Forbidden rice is a short grain black rice from China. When cooked, forbidden rice takes on a deep purple hue. If unavailable, it can be substituted with black glutinous rice or brown rice. Just soak the rice in cold water for 1 hour, then drain and prepare as with forbidden rice.

Tamarind pulp is sold in blocks, with or without seeds. To use, the pulp is soaked in water, then kneaded and strained to remove any seeds or fibres. The liquid is used to add a sour tang to dishes.

Season snapper with salt and pepper. Heat oil in a non-stick pan over medium-high heat. Place snapper skin side down in pan and cook for 2 minutes before placing in a preheated oven at 180°C (350°F) for 6 minutes. Keep warm.

Prepare forbidden rice. Place rice in a pot with water and chicken stock. Bring to a boil, then lower heat to a simmer and cover. Cook covered for 15–20 minutes before removing from heat. Leave covered for another 5 minutes so rice continues cooking in the residual heat.

Prepare tamarind banana curry. Heat butter in a pot over medium-low heat and sweat shallots until just beginning to brown. Add bananas and cook over medium-high heat until well caramelised. Takes 15–20 minutes. Sprinkle curry powder over and cook for another few minutes. Add tamarind pulp and stock and simmer for 20 minutes over low heat. Remove from heat and add lime juice and coriander leaves. Place mixture in a blender (food processor), then strain through a fine mesh sieve. Season with salt and pepper.

Prepare vegetables. Heat oil over high heat until smoking, then add baby choy sum and mushrooms. Stir-fry briefly before adding red capsicums. Season with salt and pepper.

Serve fish with forbidden rice, vegetables and lotus root chips if desired. Drizzle tamarind banana curry over.

## Hawaiian Onaga Kama with Truffle-Yaki Sauce, Sake-Braised Vegetables, Wasabi Oil and Lotus Root Chips

Preparation Time: 2 hours   Cooking Time: 1 hour 30 minutes   Serves 4

### SAKE SOY POACHING LIQUID

Sake *500 ml (20 fl oz / 2¹/2 cups)*

Mirin (see Note on pg 17) *1 litre (32 fl oz / 4 cups)*

Japanese soy sauce *375ml (12 fl oz / 1¹/2 cups)*

Fine sugar *250 g (9 oz)*

Dashi powder *2 Tbsp*

Young ginger *55 g (2 oz), peeled, sliced and pounded*

### ONAGA KAMA

Yuzu juice *125 ml (4 fl oz / ¹/2 cup)*

Onaga kama (see Note on pg 53) *4, each about 150 g (5¹/3 oz)*

Onaga fillets *4, each about 80 g (3 oz)*

Fine salt *¹/4 tsp*

Coarsely ground black pepper *¹/2 tsp*

Olive oil *2 Tbsp*

### VEGETABLE ROLLS

Daikon (white radish) *250 g (9 oz), cut into pieces, each 9 cm x 2.5 cm (3¹/2 in x 1 in)*

Carrots *140 g (5 oz), peeled and cut lengthwise into 0.5-cm (¹/4-in) thick pieces*

Russet potatoes *250 g (9 oz), peeled and cut lengthwise into 0.5-cm (¹/4-in) thick pieces*

White onions *125 g (4¹/2 oz), cut into 0.5-cm (¹/4-in) cubes*

Thai asparagus *4 spears, peeled and trimmed (see Kitchen Techniques)*

Nori (Japanese seaweed) *4 sheets*

### TRUFFLE-YAKI SAUCE

Daikon (white radish) *55 g (2 oz), finely diced (brunoise)*

Black Périgord truffle (see Glossary) *15 g (¹/2 oz), finely sliced*

Yuzu juice *60 ml (2 fl oz / ¹/4 cup)*

### LOTUS ROOT CHIPS

Lotus root *55 g (2 oz), peeled and thinly sliced*

Canola oil *180 ml (6 fl oz / ³/4 cup)*

Plain (all-purpose) flour *45 g (1¹/2 oz)*

Kosher salt *1 tsp*

### GARNISH

Organic wasabi oil *45 ml (1¹/2 fl oz / 3 Tbsp)*

Lemon *1, juice extracted*

Chervil

**NOTE**

Yuzu is a very sour Japanese citrus fruit that tastes like a mixture of lemon and lime. If the fruit is not available for extracting the juice, replace with a mixture of lemon and lime juices. Yuzu juice is also available bottled.

Wasabi oil is available in Japanese gourmet stores. It is a very fiery hot oil that has been flavoured with wasabi (Japanese horseradish) extract.

Prepare sake soy poaching liquid. Combine all ingredients and mix well.

Prepare *onaga kama*. Pour 300 ml (10 fl oz / 1¹/4 cups) sake soy poaching liquid into a bowl and add yuzu juice. Place *onaga kama* in to marinate for about 30 minutes, turning them over frequently. Remove from marinade and season *onaga kama* and fillets with salt, pepper and olive oil.

Preheat oven to 200°C (400°F) and place *onaga kama* and fillets on a baking rack over a baking tray. Bake for 6 minutes. Remove fillets and turn *onaga kama* over on rack. Continue to bake *onaga kama* for another 6 minutes or until medium.

Prepare vegetable rolls. Place remaining sake soy poaching liquid into a pan, add daikon and simmer for 15 minutes. Remove daikon and set aside to cool. Poach (see Note on pg 24) carrots, russet potatoes and onions separately until soft, then remove and set aside to cool. Reserve sake soy poaching liquid for truffle-yaki sauce.

Steam asparagus for 2 minutes and set aside to cool.

When all vegetables are cool enough to handle, place onto absorbent paper to remove excess moisture.

Lay a sheet of nori on a clean dry surface. Place 1 portion of each vegetable on top and roll nori up. Sit roll on loose edge of nori to seal. Repeat to make 4 rolls. Using a very sharp knife, cut into desired thickness. Cover with plastic wrap (cling film) and set aside.

For truffle-yaki sauce, strain reserved sake soy poaching liquid through a fine mesh sieve to get about 200 ml (6²/3 fl oz) liquid. Reduce to half over medium heat. Add daikon and simmer for 3–4 minutes, then add truffle and yuzu juice. Set aside until required.

Prepare lotus root chips. Blanch (see Note pn pg 31) lotus root slices, then drain and pat dry. Heat oil to 180°C (350°F). Dust lotus root slices with flour and deep-fry until golden brown. Drain and place onto absorbent paper. Season with salt and keep warm.

Serve *onaga kama* and fillets with vegetable rolls and truffle-yaki sauce. Drizzle with wasabi oil and lemon juice. Garnish with lotus root chips and chervil. Serve immediately.

# Shellfish

Shellfish are amongst the most treasured of foods, offering an amazing range of culinary possibilities and often reserved for meals on special days, be it a holiday celebration or a special occasion. *Naturally Peninsula – Flavours* provides a rich harvest of shellfish recipes from the simply delicious Wok-Fried Mussels with Lemon Grass and Grilled Ciabatta to the more intricate and unusual Lobster Kataifi with Virgin Mojito Shooter and Habanero Chilli. Other exquisite delicacies from the sea featured in this chapter include prawns (shrimps), scallops and soft shell crab, all of which are prepared with specific techniques and styles to accentuate their unique characteristics. Layer upon layer of mouth-watering shellfish dishes are revealed, from the traditional village-inspired *Sinigang Na Sugpo* of tiger prawns simmered in a sweet and sour tamarind broth, to the lush texture and naturally sweet flavour of diver scallops accented by a delicate lemon thyme crust, to the wonderful contrast of taste and texture captured in Soft Shell Crab with Mango and Pear Chutney.

## Cardamom-Scented Grilled Lobster

Preparation Time: 1 hour   Cooking Time: 40 minutes   Serves 4

### POTATOES

Purple or white potatoes *340 g (12 oz)*

Extra virgin olive oil *720 ml (24 fl oz / 3 cups)*

### CARDAMOM BUTTER

Cardamom seeds *1/2 Tbsp (removed from whole pods)*

Butter *30 g (1 oz), softened*

Fine salt *1/8 tsp*

Ground black pepper *1/8 tsp*

### LOBSTERS

Lobsters *4, each about 480 g (1 lb 1 1/2 oz)*

Fine salt *1/8 tsp*

Ground black pepper *1/8 tsp*

### APPLE-GINGER EMULSION

Large apples *2, about 450 g (1 lb) in total, peeled, cored and cut into chunks*

Ginger *30 g (1 oz), peeled and grated*

Water *435 ml (14 fl oz / 1 3/4 cups)*

Cold butter *30 g (1 oz)*

Salt *1/2 tsp*

### GARNISH

Mache *a handful of leaves*

Radicchio *2 leaves, cut into fine julienne*

### NOTE

Mache is also known as lamb's lettuce, with small round leaves that have a tangy, nutty flavour. It is used raw for salads or steamed as a side of vegetables.

Radicchio or red-leaved Italian chicory is a mildly bitter vegetable with firm leaves. Some varieties include radicchio di Verona which looks like a small head of red lettuce and radicchio di Treviso that looks like a red version of Belgium endive.

Froth — when recipes call for frothing up a liquid, you will need to beat the liquid with a hand-held electric blender to introduce air bubbles into the liquid. To do this, hold the blender at an angle such that not all of the paddle is in the liquid. This helps introduce air into the liquid as the paddles move, creating foam.

Prepare potatoes 1 hour before serving. Leave skin on potatoes but scrub well in cold water. Slice and place in a pot. Add extra virgin olive oil and slowly bring oil to a bare simmer. Let oil gently simmer for about 30 minutes until potatoes are slightly tender. Remove potatoes from heat and leave to cool in pot. Drain potatoes and keep warm in an oven or under a salamander while preparing rest of dish.

Crack cardamom seeds roughly and place on a sheet pan. Toast in a preheated oven at 135°C (275°F) until seeds turn light brown and are fragrant. Takes 4–5 minutes. Mix toasted cardamom seeds with softened butter and season with salt and pepper. Set aside.

Remove lobster tails and claws from body (see Kitchen Techniques). Bring a pot of lightly salted water to a boil and cook tails for 2 minutes. Remove tails and place in ice water. In the same pot of salted water, boil claws for 4 minutes. Remove claws and place in ice water. When tails and claws are chilled, remove meat from shells. Meat should appear in a raw-like state.

Toss tail and claw meat in cardamom butter and season with salt and pepper. Using a grill, cook claws for 1 minute on each side on high heat. Cook tails on each side for 1 1/2 minutes.

Place apple, ginger and water in a pot and warm over low heat for about 5 minutes. Place mixture in a blender (food processor) and purée. Pass through a fine mesh sieve to obtain juice. Discard residue. When ready to serve, heat juice, butter and salt together. Using a hand-held blender, blend mixture until froth appears.

Serve lobsters with potatoes topped with froth rendered from apple-ginger emulsion. Garnish with mache lettuce and radicchio.

## Diver Scallops Dusted with Lemon Thyme Crust, Citrus Salad and Pomegranate Reduction

Preparation Time: 30 minutes   Cooking Time: 35 minutes   Serves 4

### LEMON THYME CRUST

**Lemon grass** *1 stalk, ends trimmed, hard outer leaves removed, use only bulbous end, finely chopped*

**Lemon thyme or thyme** *30 g (1 oz), chopped*

**Lemon zest** *grated from 1 lemon*

**Japanese breadcrumbs (panko)** *30 g (1 oz)*

### DIVER SEA SCALLOPS

**Diver sea scallops or any scallops** *12*

**Fine salt** *1/2 tsp*

**Ground white pepper** *1/4 tsp*

**Olive oil** *2 tsp*

### POMEGRANATE REDUCTION

**Pomegranates (see Glossary)** *2*

**Orange** *1/2, juice extracted*

**Grapefruit** *1/2, juice extracted*

### CITRUS SALAD

**Water** *1 litre (32 fl oz / 4 cups)*

**Sugar** *800 g (1³/4 lb)*

**White vinegar** *2 Tbsp*

**Orange** *1, peeled and cut into 12 segments*

**Grapefruit** *1, peeled and cut into 12 segments*

### GARNISH

**Frisée (see Glossary)** *24 leaves*

**Mache (see Note on pg 64)** *24 leaves*

**NOTE**
Lemon thyme is similar to common or garden thyme except that it has a distinctive citrus aroma and flavour. If not available, use common thyme with a dash of lemon juice.

Prepare lemon thyme crust. Combine lemon grass, lemon thyme or thyme, lemon zest and breadcrumbs, mixing well. Set aside.

Season scallops with salt and pepper. Heat oil in a pan and sauté scallops over high heat for 2 minutes on each side. Preheat oven to 180°C (350°F) and bake scallops for 4 minutes. Remove scallops from oven and sprinkle lemon thyme crust over scallops. Place under a hot grill until golden brown. Set aside.

Prepare pomegranate reduction. Scoop out pomegranate seeds and reserve some for garnish. Extract juices from remaining seeds by squeezing seeds with hands. Combine pomegranate, orange and grapefruit juices in a pot and reduce over low heat until syrupy. Set aside.

Prepare citrus salad. Place water and sugar in a saucepot and bring to a boil. Once it comes to a boil, lower heat and simmer for another 10 minutes. Add vinegar and bring to a boil. Pour sugar-vinegar syrup over orange and grapefruit segments and toss well.

Serve scallops with drained citrus segments, topped with frisée and mache and drizzled with pomegranate reduction. Garnish with reserved pomegranate seeds.

## Wholewheat Tagliatelle with Shellfish

Preparation Time: 1 hour 30 minutes   Cooking Time: 20 minutes   Serves 4

### PASTA

**Fine salt** *1/2 tsp*

**Warm water** *1–2 Tbsp*

**Olive oil** *1 Tbsp*

**Egg yolks** *125 g (4 1/2 oz)*

**Wholewheat durum flour** *145 g (5 1/2 oz)*

### SHELLFISH HERB JUS

**Dry white wine** *215 ml (7 fl oz)*

**Garlic** *1 clove, peeled and crushed*

**Onions** *100 g (3 1/2 oz), peeled and sliced*

**Thyme** *1 sprig*

**Bay leaf** *1*

**White peppercorns** *10, crushed*

**Live mussels** *300 g (10 1/2 oz), scrubbed thoroughly and debearded; discard any open mussels*

**Live clams** *300 g (10 1/2 oz)*

**Live scallops** *8, shucked and cut into 1-cm (1/2-in) cubes*

**Chives** *10 sprigs, finely sliced*

**Dill** *2 sprigs, chopped*

**Chervil** *4 sprigs, chopped*

**Flat-leaf (Italian) parsley (see Glossary)** *3 sprigs, chopped*

**Lemon juice** *1/2 tsp*

**Olive oil** *2 tsp*

**NOTE**

Al dente is an Italian phrase that means "to the tooth". To cook food al dente means to cook it such that the food is not overdone, and is still slightly firm to the bite.

Prepare pasta. Dissolve salt in warm water, then add olive oil and egg yolks and blend well. Pass mixture through a fine mesh sieve. Place flour in a blender (food processor) or in an electric mixer with a dough hook and gradually add egg yolk mixture to achieve a smooth dough. Takes 2–3 minutes. Remove dough and knead by hand to further smoothen dough. Add a little water if necessary. Cover with plastic wrap (cling film) and allow to rest for 1 hour before using. Dust rested dough with flour and roll to 0.2-cm (1/8-in) thickness using a rolling pin or pasta machine. Cut to desired length and width.

Prepare shellfish herb jus. Bring white wine, garlic, onion, thyme, bay leaf and white peppercorns to a rapid boil, then lower heat and simmer for 10 minutes. Strain into a clean pot and return to a boil. Add mussels and clams to pot and cover with a lid. Once shells start to open, remove from heat and add scallops. Cover and leave for 30 seconds to cook scallops. Pour contents into a large colander with another pot below to capture liquid. Add chopped herbs, lemon juice and olive oil to liquid. Keep warm.

Bring a pot of lightly salted water to a boil. Lower pasta in to cook for 4 minutes until al dente. Drain well.

Return mussels, clam and scallops to shellfish herb jus to warm slightly, then toss with pasta. Garnish as desired and serve immediately.

## Wok-Fried Mussels with Lemon Grass and Grilled Ciabatta

Preparation Time: 30 minutes   Cooking Time: 20 minutes   Serves 4

### MUSSELS

Olive oil *3 Tbsp*

Lemon grass *1 stalk, ends trimmed, hard outer leaves removed, use only bulbous end, thinly sliced on a bias*

Garlic *6 cloves, peeled and minced*

Red Thai bird's eye chilli (see Glossary) *1, chopped*

Prince Edward Island mussels *2 kg (4 lb 6 oz), scrubbed thoroughly and debearded, discard any open mussels*

White wine *375 ml (12 fl oz / 1¹/₂ cups)*

Chicken stock (see pg 171) *125 ml (4 fl oz / ¹/₂ cup)*

Fine salt *³/₄ tsp*

Ground black pepper *¹/₄ tsp*

### GRILLED CIABATTA

Thyme, parsley and basil leaves *1 Tbsp in total, equal amounts of each herb, finely chopped*

Olive oil *60 ml (2 fl oz / 4 Tbsp)*

Ciabatta bread *4 slices*

Fine salt *¹/₈ tsp*

Ground black pepper *¹/₈ tsp*

Heat olive oil in a wok and sweat (see Note on pg 20) lemon grass and minced garlic for 1 minute over medium-high heat. Add chilli and mussels, tossing consistently for 1 minute over high heat. Deglaze (see Note on pg 54) with white wine and chicken stock. Cover and cook until mussels open. Takes 3–4 minutes. Remove from heat and season with salt and pepper. Keep warm.

Prepare ciabatta. Combine chopped herbs and olive oil. Brush ciabatta with herb oil and place on grill for 30 seconds. Serve with mussels.

*Photograph on facing page*

## Soft Shell Crab with Mango and Pear Chutney

Preparation Time: 40 minutes   Cooking Time: 30 minutes   Serves 4

### SOFT SHELL CRAB

Soft shell crabs *4, each about 85 g (3 oz)*

Plain (all-purpose) flour *30 g (1 oz)*

Ground paprika *10 g (¹/₃ oz)*

Eggs *2*

Fine salt *³/₄ tsp*

Ground white pepper *¹/₄ tsp*

Vegetable oil *2 litres (64 fl oz / 8 cups)*

### MANGO AND PINEAPPLE COMPOTE

Pineapple flesh *85 g (3 oz), diced*

Pear *45 g (1³/₄ oz), peeled and diced*

Mango flesh *45 g (1¹/₂ oz), diced*

Coriander leaves (cilantro) *15 g (¹/₂ oz), finely chopped*

Shallots *30 g (1 oz), peeled and left whole*

White vinegar *125 ml (4 fl oz / ¹/₂ cup)*

Lemon juice *45 ml (1¹/₂ fl oz / 3 Tbsp)*

Sugar *85 g (3 oz)*

Fine salt *¹/₈ tsp*

Ground black pepper *¹/₈ tsp*

### YOGHURT MINT DRESSING

Plain yoghurt *180 ml (6 fl oz / ³/₄ cup)*

Mint leaves *16, cut into fine julienne*

Lime zest *grated from 1 lime*

Organic honey *4 tsp*

Fine salt *¹/₈ tsp*

Ground black pepper *¹/₈ tsp*

**NOTE**
A compote is fruit cooked in sugar syrup. Compotes may also contain spices like cinnamon and cloves.

To test if the oil is heated sufficiently for deep-frying, drop some batter into the heated oil. The oil should sizzle and the batter should rise up immediately to the surface.

Cut each crab into desired serving-size pieces and pat dry with paper towels. Combine flour, paprika and eggs to form a batter. Season with salt and pepper. Heat oil over high heat. Dip crabs into batter and deep-fry for about 3 minutes, or until crabs are golden brown. Reduce heat halfway through cooking to medium to prevent crabs from over-browning. Drain crabs and set aside on paper towels. Leave aside deep-frying oil as it will be used again later.

In a small saucepan, combine ingredients for mango and pineapple compote and simmer for 15 minutes. Leave to cool. Drain before serving.

Combine ingredients for yoghurt mint dressing in a bowl. Taste and add extra seasoning of *salt* and pepper if needed. Set aside.

Just before serving, reheat oil for frying crabs. Deep-fry crabs briefly to refresh. Drain well. Serve crabs with compote and yoghurt mint dressing. Sprinkle *shichimi togarashi* (see Note on pg 17) or Japanese seven-spice seasoning over, if desired.

*Photograph on pg 72–73*

## Tiger Prawns Simmered in Tamarind Broth (Sinigang Na Sugpo)
Preparation Time: 20 minutes   Cooking Time: 35 minutes   Serves 4

**TAMARIND BROTH**

Tamarind pulp (see Note on pg 59) *30 g (1 oz), weighed without seeds*

Water *1 litre (32 fl oz / 4 cups)*

Canola oil *2 tsp*

**PRAWNS**

Canola oil *2 tsp*

Tomatoes *140 g (5 oz), cut into quarters*

Onions *125 g (4¹/₂ oz), peeled and cut into quarters*

Tiger prawns (shrimps) *480 g (16 oz), peeled, leaving tails intact and heads on 4 prawns, shells reserved*

Chilli fingers or red chillies *30 g (1 oz), left whole*

Green (string) beans *100 g (3¹/₃ oz), ends trimmed, cut into 5-cm (2-in) lengths*

White cabbage *100 g (3¹/₃ oz), sliced diagonally*

Fine salt *1 tsp*

Ground white pepper *¹/₂ tsp*

Kalamansi limes (see Glossary) *4, each cut in half*

**NOTE**

Chilli fingers are from the Philippines. They are plump and about the length of a thumb. Chilli fingers are usually sold when ripe and red. If unavailable, replace with large red chillies.

Prepare tamarind broth. Mix tamarind pulp with water and knead well to incorporate tamarind into water. Strain. Heat oil and sauté reserved prawn shells over medium heat for 3–4 minutes. Pour in tamarind water and bring to a boil. Lower heat and simmer for about 20 minutes. Strain and set aside.

Prepare prawns. Heat oil and sauté tomatoes and onions until onions are translucent. Deglaze (see note on pg 54) with tamarind broth and simmer for about 10 minutes. Add prawns, chillies and green beans. Bring to a boil for 1 minute before adding cabbage. Cover and simmer for another 5 minutes. Season with salt and pepper.

Spoon tamarind broth over prawns and vegetables and serve with a squeeze of lime juice. Garnish as desired.

## Lobster Kataifi with Virgin Mojito Shooter and Habanero Chilli

Preparation Time: 30 minutes   Cooking Time: 45 minutes   Serves 4

### VIRGIN MOJITO

Sugar *2 tsp*

Water *1 Tbsp*

Orange *1, juice extracted*

Lime juice *3 Tbsp*

Pineapple juice *2 Tbsp*

Lemon juice *1 Tbsp*

Crushed ice *2 Tbsp*

Mint leaves *16*

### HABANERO CHILLI SAUCE

Red capsicums (bell peppers) *400 g*
  *(14$^1$/$_3$ oz), cored, seeded and chopped*

Water *90 ml (3 fl oz/ 6 Tbsp)*

Habanero chilli powder *1 Tbsp*

Olive oil *90 ml (3 fl oz / 6 Tbsp)*

Fine salt *$^1$/$_8$ tsp*

Ground black pepper *$^1$/$_8$ tsp*

### LOBSTER KATAIFI

Lobster tail meat *from 4 tails, each 45–60 g*
  *(1$^1$/$_2$–2 oz) (see Kitchen Techniques)*

Fine salt *$^1$/$_4$ tsp*

Ground black pepper *$^1$/$_8$ tsp*

Kataifi pastry *55 g (2 oz)*

Canola oil *1 litre (32 fl oz / 4 cups)*

**NOTE**

Mojito is a traditional Cuban cocktail made with 5 main ingredients — mint, sugar, lime juice, rum and club soda. Virgin mojito is a non-alcoholic version of the Cuban classic.

Habanero chillies are among the hottest chillies in the world. They are available in both fresh and dried forms. If unavailable, use any hot chilli powder.

Kataifi dough comes commercially packaged as long, fine strands of shredded filo pastry. To prepare it for this recipe, lay the dough on a clean work surface and divide the strands into separate portions, gently spreading the strands out a bit if they clump together. Each portion will be used to create an individual lobster kataifi roll. Keep unused dough covered with a piece of waxed paper and damp towel to keep from drying out.

Prepare Virgin Mojito. Melt sugar in water, then combine all ingredients in a blender (food processor) and blend until well mixed. Set aside.

Prepare chilli sauce. Place capsicums and water in a blender (food processor) and blend into a purée. Strain for juice and discard pulp. Place juice and chilli powder in a pan over low heat, stirring until mixture starts to thicken. Strain through a chinois and leave to cool. When cool, stir in oil to achieve a dressing-like consistency. Season with salt and pepper. Set aside.

Prepare lobster kataifi. Season lobster meat with salt and pepper and wrap with pastry. Heat oil and deep-fry wrapped lobster over high heat using tongs to hold lobster straight.

Place lobster kataifi into glasses with Virgin Mojito and serve with chilli sauce. Garnish as desired.

# Poultry

From chicken and duck to squab and quail, these succulent birds pack in deeply intense flavours. Here, they are presented in an enticing array of recipes, from the hot and fiery Thai tastes of *Gaeng Pa Gai* to the sweet and tart flavours of Roasted Duck with Lemon-Honey Glaze and Spiced Cherries and the light and delicate Cantonese-inspired Steamed Sliced Chicken with Black Mushrooms and Chestnuts. This high-quality protein food is also nutrient-dense, making it a great choice for meat protein. With thoughtfully-composed side elements and garnishes which offer support by way of contrasting textures and flavours, the *Naturally Peninsula* poultry dishes run the gamut from light to rich, mellow to robust, and each will stimulate and satiate your appetite in its own spectacular and characteristic way!

## Grilled Organic Quail with Warm Cucumber and Daikon Salad
Preparation Time: 2 hours (prepare a day ahead)   Cooking Time: 30 minutes   Serves 4

### VINAIGRETTE

Olive oil *1 Tbsp*

Ginger *15 g (¹/₂ oz), peeled and finely chopped*

Shallots *3, peeled and sliced*

Curry leaves *12*

Maharaja curry powder *55 g (2 oz)*

Grapeseed oil *250 ml (8 fl oz / 1 cup)*

White balsamic vinegar *85 ml (2¹/₂ fl oz / ¹/₃ cup)*

Lemon zest *1 tsp*

Lemon juice *2 Tbsp*

Fine salt *¹/₈ tsp*

Ground black pepper *¹/₈ tsp*

### QUAIL

Semi-boneless organic quails *4, each about 160 g (5¹/₂ oz)*

Ginger *10 g (¹/₃ oz), peeled and minced*

Garlic *1 clove, peeled and minced*

Grapeseed or olive oil *250 ml (8 fl oz / 1 cup)*

Lemon juice *1 Tbsp*

Fine salt *¹/₂ tsp*

Ground white pepper *¹/₄ tsp*

### CUCUMBER SALAD

Olive oil *1 tsp*

Shallots *2, peeled and chopped*

English cucumbers (see Note on pg 40) *210 g (7¹/₂ oz), peeled, seeded and diced*

Pickled daikon (white radish) *85 g (3 oz), diced*

Red capsicums (bell peppers) *85 g (3 oz), cored, seeded and diced*

Fine salt *¹/₈ tsp*

Ground black pepper *¹/₈ tsp*

### CAPSICUM REDUCTION

Red capsicums (bell peppers) *300 g (10 oz), cored, seeded and roughly chopped*

Water *2 Tbsp*

Organic honey *1 Tbsp*

### GARNISH

English cucumber *1, thinly sliced lengthwise*

Salad leaves

**NOTE**
Maharajah curry powder is a rich mixture of spices usually consisting of turmeric, coriander, cumin, cardamom, fenugreek, ginger, nutmeg, fennel, cinnamon, white, black and red peppercorns, cloves and saffron. If unavailable, use a curry powder for meat.

Prepare vinaigrette a day ahead. Heat olive oil in a saucepot and sauté ginger and shallots over medium heat. Add curry leaves and curry powder and cook over medium-low heat for 1 minute. Add grapeseed oil and stir. Bring oil to 100°C (210°F), then remove and set aside in a warm place for 24 hours, stirring occasionally. Let sit for another hour to allow sediment to settle. Gently ladle oil into a separate container, leaving sediment behind. Place balsamic vinegar, lemon zest and juice into a bowl and slowly whisk in oil. Season with salt and pepper. Set aside.

Rinse quails, pat dry and place into a bowl. Add ginger, garlic, oil and lemon juice and leave to marinate for 2 hours, covered with plastic wrap (cling film). When ready, season quails with salt and pepper. Grill over medium-high heat for 3 minutes on each side until medium. Grill for a longer time if you prefer the quails more fully cooked.

Prepare cucumber salad. Heat olive oil and sauté shallots over medium-high heat until translucent. Add diced vegetables and continue to sauté for 2–3 minutes over medium heat. Add 60 ml (2 fl oz / 4 Tbsp) vinaigrette and season with salt and pepper, tossing to mix well. Set aside.

Prepare capsicum reduction. Place capsicum and water into a blender (food processor) and purée. Place purée into a small saucepot and cook for 5 minutes. Pass through a fine mesh sieve, then return juice to saucepot. Stir in honey and reduce to about 3 Tbsp over low heat. Transfer to a small bowl and leave to cool.

Serve quails with cucumber salad and capsicum reduction. Garnish with thinly sliced cucumber and salad leaves if desired.

## Peking Duck Rolls with Roasted Pineapple

Preparation Time: 30 minutes   Cooking Time: 5 minutes   Serves 4

**Peking duck breast or Chinese roast duck breast** *200 g (7 oz)*

**Chinese sweet soy bean paste** *60 ml (2 fl oz / 4 Tbsp)*

**Pineapple flesh** *85 g (3 oz), thinly sliced*

**Vietnamese rice paper** *8 sheets*

**Cucumber** *85 g (3 oz), peeled and cut into fine julienne*

**Red capsicums (bell pepper)** *45 g (1 1/2 oz), cored, seeded and cut into fine julienne*

**Hoisin sauce** *2 Tbsp*

**Water** *2 tsp*

**Mustard sprouts** *85 g (3 oz)*

**Pea shoot leaves** *45 g (1 1/2 oz)*

Remove crispy duck skin from duck. Trim fat and discard. Cut skin into small pieces. Set aside.

Shred duck breast meat into fine julienne. Mix with sweet soy bean paste.

Grill pineapple slices until nicely brown. Takes about 5 minutes.

To assemble, soak a sheet of rice paper in cold water until soft, then spread out on a kitchen towel to absorb excess liquid. Arrange some duck meat, roasted pineapple, cucumber and capsicum on rice paper and roll up to form a small spring roll-shaped parcel. Repeat to make 8 parcels. Arrange rolls on a serving plate.

Mix hoisin sauce with water to thin the sauce.

Serve duck rolls with duck skin and sauce. Garnish with mustard sprouts, pea shoot leaves and any remaining pineapple.

## Pan-Seared Squab Breast, Chanterelles and Baby Leeks with Port Wine-Lime Jus

Preparation Time: 30 minutes   Cooking Time: 2 hours   Serves 4

**Squabs** *2, each about 450 g (1 lb)*

**Olive oil** *2 Tbsp*

**Garlic** *1 head, cut horizontally in half*

**Shallots** *110 g (4 oz), peeled and chopped*

**Carrots** *55 g (2 oz), peeled and chopped*

**Celery** *55 g (2 oz), chopped*

**Lime juice** *125 ml (4 fl oz / 1/2 cup)*

**Port wine** *60 ml (2 fl oz / 4 Tbsp)*

**Veal stock (see pg 171)** *1 litre (32 fl oz / 4 cups)*

**Fine salt** *1 tsp*

**Ground black pepper** *1/2 tsp*

MUSHROOMS

**Fresh chanterelles (see Glossary)** *110 g (4 oz), or portobello (see Glossary) or oyster mushrooms, caps wiped*

**Baby leeks** *55 g (2 oz), cut into 5-cm (2-in) lengths*

**Fine salt** *1/4 tsp*

**Ground black pepper** *1/4 tsp*

**Olive oil** *1 Tbsp*

GARNISH

**Finely grated lime zest**

Remove breast meat from squabs, leaving skins intact. Cut each breast in half to get 4 pieces in total. Refrigerate.

Prepare port wine-lime jus. Heat 1 Tbsp oil and sauté squab carcasses over high heat with garlic, shallots, carrots and celery. Cook until caramelised. Deglaze (see Note on pg 54) with lime juice and port. Reduce to half over medium heat. Add stock and bring to a boil, then lower heat and simmer for 1 hour. Strain and reduce over medium heat until sauce is thick and coats the back of a spoon. Season with 1/2 tsp salt and 1/4 tsp pepper. Keep warm.

Remove squab breasts from refrigerator and season with remaining salt and pepper. Heat remaining oil and sear squab breasts over high heat for 2–3 minutes until golden brown on both sides. Roast in a preheated oven at 270°C (520°F) for 4 minutes.

Prepare mushrooms. Season mushrooms and leeks with salt and pepper. Heat oil and sauté quickly over high heat until cooked. Takes 2–3 minutes.

Blanch (see Note on pg 31) lime zest for garnish. Drain and refresh in ice water. Drain before using.

Serve squabs with mushrooms, leeks and port wine-lime jus. Garnish with lime zest.

## Organic Chicken with Thai Red Curry Paste and Chinese Key (Gaeng Pa Gai)

Preparation Time: 20 minutes  Cooking Time: 20 minutes  Serves 4

Thai red curry paste *45 g (1¹/₂ oz)*

Organic chicken breast *320 g (11 oz),
trimmed and cut into bite-size pieces*

Chicken stock (see pg 171) *800 ml
(26 fl oz / 3¹/₄ cups)*

Baby corn *55 g (2 oz), cut diagonally in half*

Long beans *55 g (2 oz), cut into 2-cm
(1-in) lengths*

Straw mushrooms (see Glossary) *55 g (2 oz),
each cut in half*

Aubergines (eggplants) *55 g (2 oz), sliced*

Chinese key (krachai) *20 g (²/₃ oz), peeled
and sliced*

Fish sauce *30–60 ml (1–2 fl oz / 2–4 Tbsp),
or to taste*

Sugar *3 Tbsp*

Red Thai bird's eye chillies (see Glossary)
*20 g (²/₃ oz), sliced*

Fresh green peppercorns *20 g (²/₃ oz)*

Kaffir lime leaves (see Glossary) *15,
crushed*

Hot basil leaves (see Glossary) *20 g (²/₃ oz)*

### GARNISH

Tempura long bean (see pg 54)

Red chilli *1, seeded and cut into
fine julienne*

Coriander leaves (cilantro)

**NOTE**

Chinese key (*krachai*) is also known as lesser ginger and is made up of a cluster of finger-like tubers sprouting from a central knob. This rhizome is an important ingredient in Thai cooking, used primarily in seafood dishes to freshen the taste of the seafood with its distinctive piquant flavour and tangy fragrance.

Thai red curry paste is readily available in supermarkets around the world. It is pre-fried in oil, so there is no need to use additional oil when refrying the paste to refresh the flavours.

Stir-fry red curry paste over medium heat until fragrant, then add chicken, stirring all the while. Add 250 ml (8 fl oz / 1 cup) chicken stock and bring to a boil. When boiling, add baby corn, long beans, mushrooms, aubergines and Chinese key. Return to a boil and add remaining chicken stock.

Add fish sauce to taste, sugar, chillies, peppercorns, kaffir lime leaves and hot basil leaves and return to a boil. When boiling, remove from heat.

Garnish with tempura long bean, chilli and coriander, if desired, and serve hot with steamed rice.

## Steamed Sliced Chicken with Black Mushrooms and Chestnuts

Start preparations 6 hours ahead   Cooking Time: 20 minutes   Serves 4

**Chestnuts** *85 g (3 oz)*

**Dried Chinese black mushrooms** *30 g (1 oz), soaked in warm water for 4–6 hours to soften, then drained*

**Chicken breast** *450 g (16 oz), skinned and trimmed*

**Oyster sauce** *4 tsp*

**Fine salt** *$1/4$–$1/2$ tsp*

**Sugar** *1 tsp*

**White turnip** *30 g (1 oz), peeled and sliced*

**Choy sum, Hong Kong variety** *30 g (1 oz)*

**Sugar snap peas or snow peas** *30 g (1 oz)*

Shell chestnuts and make a slit in the skin. Cook in boiling water for 6–8 minutes until soft. Peel off and discard skin.

Cut hard stems from mushrooms and slice caps in half on the diagonal.

Season chicken with oyster sauce, salt and sugar and place in a deep steaming dish. Steam over high heat for 4 minutes. Add turnip, choy sum and peas, then turn chicken over and steam for another 5 minutes until chicken is cooked. Strain steaming juices and reserve.

Slice chicken and serve with chestnuts, mushrooms, turnip, choy sum and peas. Drizzle with strained juices.

# Roasted Duck with Lemon-Honey Glaze and Spiced Cherries

Preparation Time: 1 hour (prepare a day ahead)   Cooking Time: 1 hour   Serves 4

Duck breasts 4, each 180–200 g (6$^1$/$_2$–7 oz)

### SPICED CHERRIES

Pineau des Charentes 100 ml (3$^1$/$_3$ fl oz)

Red wine 200 ml (7 fl oz / $^4$/$_5$ cup)

Port wine 200 ml (7 fl oz / $^4$/$_5$ cup)

Cinnamon stick 3-cm (1$^1$/$_4$-in) length

Cloves 1 tsp

Black peppercorns 1 tsp

Thyme 1 sprig

Bay leaf 1

Garlic 1 clove

Cherries 200 g (7 oz), pitted

### LEMON-HONEY GLAZE

Lemon juice 90 ml (3 fl oz / 6 Tbsp)

Orange juice 60 ml (2 fl oz / 4 Tbsp)

Sherry vinegar 125 ml (4 fl oz / $^1$/$_2$ cup)

Organic honey 250 ml (8 fl oz / 1 cup)

Ground cinnamon 10 g ($^1$/$_3$ oz)

Ground cloves 10 g ($^1$/$_3$ oz)

Salt $^1$/$_8$ tsp

Ground black pepper 1 Tbsp

### WILD MUSHROOMS

Olive oil 1 Tbsp

Seasonal mushrooms 30 g (1 oz), trimmed
   and cleaned

Fine salt $^1$/$_8$ tsp

Ground black pepper $^1$/$_8$ tsp

### LETTUCE

Olive oil 1 Tbsp

Romaine lettuce 100 g (3$^1$/$_2$ oz)

Fine salt $^1$/$_8$ tsp

Ground black pepper $^1$/$_8$ tsp

**NOTE**

Pineau des Charentes is an aperitif from France made from Cognac eau de vie and grape juice which come from the same property and have been aged in oak casks for at least 18 months.

To render fat means to cook the raw, fatty part of the meat touching the hot pan so that the oil is extracted from the solid fat. After the oil is rendered, what remains is a crisp skin with a delicious smoky flavour.

Prepare spiced cherries a day ahead. Reduce Pineau des Charentes, red wine and port each by half separately. Combine in a saucepan and add remaining ingredients except cherries. Bring to a boil. When boiling, add cherries and simmer over medium-low heat for 4 minutes. Remove from heat and leave cherries to cool in sauce. Cover and refrigerate for 12 hours.

Carefully remove all traces of sinew, excess skin and fat from duck breasts. Score remaining skin with close, evenly spaced cuts in a criss-cross pattern. Refrain from cutting too deep into meat.

Prepare lemon-honey glaze. Combine lemon and orange juices and vinegar in a stainless steel pan and reduce over low heat to about 60 ml (2 fl oz / 4 Tbsp). Add honey and boil for 5 minutes. Add spices and stir to mix evenly. Remove from heat and season to taste with salt and pepper.

Place prepared duck breasts on a hot, dry frying pan, skin side down over medium-high heat. Render fat for about 8 minutes. Brush with a little lemon-honey glaze and roast for 6 minutes in a pre-heated oven at 180°C (350°F), skin side up. Remove and leave to rest for 10 minutes. Brush heavily with lemon-honey glaze and return to oven for another 6 minutes. Remove and leave to rest for 2 minutes before slicing and serving.

While duck is baking, heat olive oil and quickly sauté mushrooms for 2 minutes over high heat. Season with salt and pepper. Keep warm.

Prepare lettuce. Heat olive oil and sauté lettuce until wilted. Season with salt and pepper.

Serve duck with mushrooms, lettuce and spiced cherries.

## Organic Chicken Pastilla with Almonds and Cinnamon in Filo Crust

Preparation Time: 50 minutes   Cooking Time: 2 hours 30 minutes   Serves 4

### CHICKEN

Extra virgin olive oil *2 Tbsp*

Butter *30 g (1 oz)*

Boneless chicken thigh *170 g (6 oz), excess skin removed*

Boneless chicken breast *170 g (6 oz), excess skin removed*

Onions *55 g (2 oz), peeled and finely sliced*

Saffron threads *¼ tsp*

Ground white pepper *⅛ tsp*

Ground cinnamon *1½ tsp*

Sugar *1 tsp*

Ground ginger *2 tsp*

Chicken stock (see pg 171) *375 ml (12 fl oz / 1½ cups)*

Eggs *2*

Chopped flat-leaf (Italian) parsley (see Glossary) *1 Tbsp*

Breadcrumbs *70 g (2½ oz)*

Fine salt *¼ tsp*

### CHICKEN JUS

Corn oil *2 Tbsp*

Carrot *55 g (2 oz), peeled and cut into small cubes*

Onion *40 g (1⅓ oz), peeled and cut into small cubes*

Celery *45 g (1½ oz), cubed*

Garlic *10 g (⅓ oz), peeled*

Tomato paste *55 g (2 oz)*

Canned peeled tomatoes *85 g (3 oz)*

Red wine *200 ml (7 fl oz)*

Mixed fresh herbs (see pg 53) *10 g (⅓ oz)*

Chicken bones *1 kg (2 lb 3 oz)*

Water *1 litre (32 fl oz / 4 cups)*

Port wine *90 ml (3 fl oz / 6 Tbsp)*

Cold butter *30 g (1 oz)*

Fine salt *¼ tsp*

Ground white pepper *⅛ tsp*

### CHICKEN PARCELS

Filo pastry *8 sheets*

Butter *30 g (1 oz), softened at room temperature*

Almond slivers *2 Tbsp, toasted*

Dried apricots *30 g (1 oz), cut into small cubes*

Spring onions (scallions) *4, blanched*

### GARNISH

Almond slivers

Dried apricots

Raisins

Flat-leaf (Italian) parsley (see Glossary)

**NOTE**
Pastilla is also spelled as b'steeya and is a traditional Moroccan dish made with filo pastry encasing a mixture of shredded chicken, ground almonds and spices.

Prepare chicken. In stockpot, over medium heat, add olive oil and butter. When butter melts, add chicken thigh and breast and brown on all sides. Add onions, saffron, pepper, cinnamon, sugar and ginger and sauté well before adding chicken stock. Let mixture simmer on low heat for about 15 minutes until chicken is cooked. Remove chicken and continue to reduce stock to one-third over medium heat. Break eggs into a mixing bowl and beat lightly. Add eggs gradually to simmering stock. Add parsley and breadcrumbs and season with salt. Remove from heat and set aside.

Shred chicken meat into fine julienne.

Prepare chicken jus. Heat oil in a stockpot and sauté carrot, onion, celery and garlic for 2–3 minutes. Add tomato paste and canned tomatoes and sauté well. After 1 minute, deglaze (see Note on pg 54) with red wine and add herbs. Add chicken bones and water and bring to a boil. Lower heat and simmer gently for about 2 hours, constantly skimming off any impurities that rise to the surface during the process. Pass through a cloth-lined strainer. Return stock to heat, add port wine and reduce over medium heat to a glaze. Stir in cold butter, then season with salt and pepper.

Prepare chicken parcels. Lay a filo sheet on a work surface and brush with softened butter. Top with another filo sheet, then trim to get a 23-cm (9-in) square. Spoon some almonds and apricots in the centre of filo square, top with egg mixture and shredded chicken, then sprinkle with more almonds and apricots. Gather edges of filo pastry together to form a pouch and enclose filling. Secure with blanched spring onion. Brush with softened butter. Repeat to make 4 parcels. Bake parcels in a preheated oven at 180°C (350°F) for 20 minutes.

Serve chicken parcels with chicken jus. Garnish with almonds, apricots, raisins and parsley.

# Meat

Superior ingredients make for superior dishes and the *Naturally Peninsula* meat recipes focus on top-quality, prime-grade cuts of meat. Slow-Poached Grass-Fed Beef Fillet with Pot-Au-Feu of Root Vegetables and Morels features a succulent piece of beef and a colourful bouquet of vegetables cooked in a comforting and restorative broth. Beef sirloin is marinated, then grilled in *Nue Sa-Doong* and topped with a piquant hot and sour Thai sauce. The tenderness of veal is fully captured through an innovative cooking method in Slow-Cooked Veal Fillet with Green Lentils. The best cut of lamb, the loin, is offered in two different but equally vivid preparations, while Kurobuta Pork Pot Roast with Melted Vegetables, New Age Apple Sauce and Beetroot Drizzle showcases the most highly prized pork from the exquisite breed of Black Berkshire pigs.

## Lamb Loin in a Whole Grain Bread Crust, Braised Chinese Vegetables and Five Spice-Mustard Jus

Preparation Time: 30 minutes   Cooking Time: 45 minutes   Serves 4

### LAMB

Lamb loin *700 g (1¹/₂ lb), with bone, trimmed*

Sea salt *¹/₂ tsp*

Ground white pepper *¹/₂ tsp*

Mustard powder *30 g (1 oz)*

Whole grain breadcrumbs *100 g (3¹/₂ oz)*

### VEGETABLES

Chicken stock *(see pg 171) 250 ml (8 fl oz / 1 cup)*

Fine salt *¹/₂ tsp*

Ground black pepper *¹/₄ tsp*

Bok choy *320 g (10 oz)*

Edamame beans *30*

Sugar snap peas *4*

Baby carrots *60 g (2 oz)*

Seasonal mushrooms *30 g (1 oz), sliced*

Olive oil *1 tsp*

### FIVE SPICE-MUSTARD JUS

Olive oil *1 Tbsp*

Shallots *15 g (¹/₂ oz), peeled and chopped*

Champignons (button mushrooms) *30 g (1 oz), chopped*

Chinese five spice powder *1 tsp*

Lamb jus *(see pg 170) 160 ml (5 fl oz / ¹/₂ cup)*

Mustard powder *8 g (1¹/₂ tsp)*

Fine salt *³/₈ tsp*

Ground white pepper *¹/₈ tsp*

Sugar *¹/₄ tsp*

Season lamb with salt and pepper. Pan-sear over high heat for 2 minutes on each side. Toss with mustard powder and breadcrumbs, then roast in a preheated oven at 120°C (250°F) for 12 minutes. Allow to rest for at least 10 minutes before slicing and serving.

Prepare vegetables. Heat stock and season with salt and half the pepper. Poach (see Note on pg 24) bok choy, edamame beans, sugar snap peas and baby carrots. Drain and slice as desired. Set aside.

Grill sliced mushrooms with olive oil and season with remaining pepper.

Prepare five spice-mustard jus. Heat oil and sauté shallots and champignons over high heat. Add five spice powder and sauté for a few seconds, then add lamb jus and mustard powder. Simmer for a few minutes, then season with salt, pepper and sugar.

Serve lamb with vegetables, mushrooms and five spice-mustard jus. Garnish as desired.

## Grilled Beef Sirloin with Bok Choy, Garlic and Chilli-Lime Dip (Nue Sa-Doong)

Preparation Time: 30 minutes   Cooking Time: 30 minutes   Serves 4

### BEEF

**Beef sirloin** *500 g (1 lb 1½ oz), cut into 2 long pieces*

**Light soy sauce** *2 Tbsp*

**Oyster sauce** *1 Tbsp*

**Bok choy** *200 g (7 oz), cut diagonally into 3-cm (1¼-in) lengths and soaked in ice water*

**Garlic** *5 cloves, peeled, sliced and soaked in ice water*

### SAUCE

**Red Thai bird's eye chillies (see Glossary)** *10*

**Garlic** *12 cloves, peeled*

**Coriander roots** *5*

**Fish sauce** *60 ml (2 fl oz / 4 Tbsp)*

**Thin-skinned Thai lime juice** *60 ml (2 fl oz / 4 Tbsp)*

**Sugar** *60 g (2 oz)*

**NOTE**

Thin-skinned limes are much like key limes in their uniquely mild flavour. If unavailable, use juice from kalamansi limes (see Glossary).

Coriander root is the root of the coriander plant. It has a deeper and more intense flavour than the leaves and is commonly used in South East Asian cooking.

Marinate beef with light soy sauce and oyster sauce for 15–20 minutes, then grill over charcoal until medium or desired doneness. Alternatively, heat 2 Tbsp oil in a pan and sear beef over high heat for 3–4 minutes. Roast in a preheated oven at 200°C (400°F) for 10 minutes to medium or to desired doneness. Rest beef for 10 minutes, then slice thinly. Set aside on a serving plate.

Combine ingredients for sauce and blend (process) into a fine, thick sauce.

Drain bok choy and garlic.

Serve beef with bok choy and garlic, drizzled with sauce. Garnish as desired.

## Slow-Poached Grass-Fed Beef Fillet with Pot-Au-Feu of Root Vegetables and Morels

Preparation Time: 50 minutes   Cooking Time: 20 minutes   Serves 4

Veal stock (see pg 171) *750 ml (24 fl oz / 3 cups), boiling hot*

Thyme *4 sprigs*

Fine salt *1/2 tsp*

Ground black pepper *1/4 tsp*

Sea salt (optional) *1/8 tsp*

### SAUTÉED VEGETABLES

Butter *55 g (2 oz)*

Carrot *55 g (2 oz), peeled and sliced*

Red radish *55 g (2 oz), peeled and sliced*

Daikon (white radish) *55 g (2 oz), peeled and sliced*

Celeriac root (see Glossary) *55 g (2 oz), peeled and sliced*

Baby leek *85 g (3 oz), trimmed, left whole*

Dried morels (see Glossary) *45 g (1 1/2 oz), soaked to soften and squeezed dry; reserve soaking liquid*

Fine salt *1/4 tsp*

Ground black pepper *1/8 tsp*

### BEEF FILLET

Beef fillet *600 g (1 lb 5 1/3 oz), trimmed*

Fine salt *1/4 tsp*

Ground black pepper *1/8 tsp*

Canola oil *2 Tbsp*

**NOTE**

Pot-au-feu means "pot on the fire" in French. Traditionally, it refers to a French dish of meat, usually beef, and vegetables which are slowly cooked in broth.

Prepare vegetables. Heat butter in a pan and sauté vegetables and morels over high heat for 2 minutes. Season with salt and pepper. Set aside.

Season beef fillet with salt and pepper. Heat oil and pan-fry beef over high heat for about 30 seconds on each side.

Place sautéed vegetables and beef into a stockpot. Add veal stock and reserved soaking liquid for morels. Add thyme, cover and simmer over low heat for about 15 minutes until beef is cooked to medium doneness. Remove beef and let it rest for about 5 minutes before slicing. Season stock with salt and pepper.

Serve beef with sautéed vegetables and stock. Sprinkle with sea salt if desired.

## Forever Roasted Pork with Sweet Potato Mash and Young Spinach

Preparation Time: 1 hour (prepare a day ahead)   Cooking Time: 4 hours   Serves 4

### PORK

Pork shoulder *700 g (1¹/₂ lb), trimmed and skinned*

White rice vinegar *215 ml (9 fl oz)*

Dark soy sauce *90–125 ml (3–4 fl oz / ³/₈–¹/₂ cup)*

Plum sauce *215 ml (9 fl oz)*

Bay leaves *3*

Coriander seeds *85 g (3 oz), or less for a milder flavour*

Five spice powder *30 g (1 oz), or less for a milder flavour*

Mature ginger *30 g (1 oz), peeled and chopped*

Ground white pepper *¹/₄ tsp*

Fine salt *¹/₄ tsp*

### SWEET POTATO MASH

Sweet potatoes *400 g (14 oz), washed and dried*

Fine salt *¹/₈ tsp*

Ground white pepper *¹/₈ tsp*

### VEGETABLES

Butter *55 g (2 oz)*

Spinach leaves *125 g (4¹/₂ oz), weighed without stalks, sliced and blanched (see Note on pg 31)*

Fine salt *¹/₄ tsp*

Ground white pepper *¹/₈ tsp*

Baby carrots *125 g (4¹/₂ oz), peeled and blanched (see Note on pg 31)*

### SAUCE

Pineapple juice *500 ml (16 fl oz / 2 cups)*

Tomato juice *90 ml (3 fl oz / 6 Tbsp)*

Shallots *5, peeled and chopped*

Garlic *1 clove, peeled and left whole*

Coriander seeds *1 tsp*

Place pork in a large container. Combine all other ingredients for pork and pour over pork. Leave to marinate overnight, refrigerated. Place pork in large pot together with marinade and roast in an oven at 120°C (250°F) until pork is tender. Takes at least 2 hours. Continue to roast for another 1 hour 30 minutes if you prefer the pork fork-tender.

To make sweet potato mash, bake unpeeled whole sweet potatoes in a preheated oven at 180°C (350°F) for 40 minutes. When cool enough to handle, peel sweet potatoes and mash with a potato masher. Season with salt and pepper. Set aside.

Heat half the butter and sauté spinach over high heat. Season with salt and pepper. Heat remaining butter and sauté blanched carrots.

Combine ingredients for sauce in a pot and reduce by half over medium-low heat. Strain.

Slice and serve pork with sweet potato mash, spinach, carrots and sauce.

## Kurobuta Pork Pot Roast with Stewed Vegetables, New Age Apple Sauce and Beetroot Drizzle

Preparation Time: 1 hour   Cooking Time: 45 minutes   Serves 4

### KUROBUTA PORK

Kurobuta pork 700 g (1¹/₂ lb), trimmed of fat and sinew, cut into 2 steaks

Olive oil 3 Tbsp

Mixed fresh herbs (see pg 53) a large handful, plucked, washed and roughly chopped

Fine salt ¹/₄ Tbsp

Freshly ground black pepper ¹/₄ tsp

Rosemary sprigs

Tarragon sprigs

### STEWED VEGETABLES

Garlic 1 head, cut horizontally in half

Carrot 70 g (2¹/₂ oz), peeled and cut into fingers

Parsnip 70 g (2¹/₂ oz), peeled and cut into fingers

Pumpkin 70 g (2¹/₂ oz), peeled, seeded and cut into fingers

Shallots 45 g (1¹/₂ oz), peeled and left whole

Dry white wine 100 ml (3¹/₃ fl oz)

Chicken stock (see pg 171) 200 ml (6²/₃ fl oz), kept hot

Olive oil 2 tsp

Fine salt ¹/₄ tsp

Ground black pepper ¹/₄ tsp

### APPLE SAUCE

Red apples 2, peeled, cored and cut into quarters

Star anise 1

Ginger 10 g (¹/₃ oz), peeled and sliced

Apple balsamico 60 ml (2 fl oz / 4 Tbsp)

Fine salt ¹/₈ tsp

Ground black pepper ¹/₈ tsp

Lemon juice 1 tsp

### BEETROOT DRIZZLE

Beetroot 100 g (3¹/₃ oz)

Olive oil 4 tsp

Lemon juice 1 tsp

Micri 1 tsp

### NOTE

Kurobuta pork comes from pure-bred Berkshire pigs. It is priced as much as Kobe beef for its fine marbling and shorter muscle fibres, which makes it very tender and juicy.

Micri is a neutral sauce base made from cassava (manioc) and water. It is colourless and odourless and enhances the taste and aroma of sauces while adding shine. It can also be used in sorbets, ice creams and liqueurs.

Prepare pork. Tie pork steaks with string so they hold their shape. Rub steaks with some oil, then sprinkle generously with herbs, salt and pepper. Cover and leave for 1 hour, refrigerated. Heat remaining oil in a pan and sear steaks over high heat. Set aside.

Prepare stewed vegetables. Using the same pan, drain oil and sauté garlic, carrot, parsnip, pumpkin and shallots until translucent. Add half the white wine to deglaze (see Note on pg 54), then reduce completely and add remaining wine. Reduce completely once again and add hot chicken stock. Bring to a boil and reduce to two-thirds.

Place pork steaks into pan with vegetables and sauce. Cover and place in a preheated oven at 120°C (250°F) for 20 minutes to cook steaks until medium-well. Remove and place steaks in a warm place. Strain cooking jus into a clean pot and set vegetables aside.

Prepare apple sauce. Place apples in a juicer, then combine apple juice, star anise, ginger and apple balsamico with strained cooking jus from pork. Simmer over low heat until sauce is thickened, then remove star anise and ginger. Using a hand blender, blend (process) sauce until froth appears. Season with salt, pepper, lemon juice and extra apple balsamico, if desired. Keep warm.

Roast beetroot in a preheated oven at 180°C (350°F) for about 30 minutes until soft. Peel and purée into a fine mousse, then strain through a fine mesh wire sieve. Discard pulp. Add olive oil, lemon juice and micri to beetroot juice. The drizzle should be "silky" in appearance. Add more olive oil, if needed, and set aside.

Toss stewed vegetables in olive oil over medium heat and season with salt and pepper.

Use only leaves from rosemary and tarragon. Chop finely. Coat pork with chopped herbs and slice equally. Serve pork steaks with stewed vegetables, apple sauce and beetroot drizzle. Garnish as desired.

## Roast Loin of Lamb with Apricot Stuffing and Grilled Capsicums

Preparation Time: 40 minutes   Cooking Time: 50 minutes   Serves 4

### APRICOT STUFFING

**Shallots** *4, peeled and finely chopped*

**Garlic** *3 cloves, peeled and finely chopped*

**Olive oil** *1 Tbsp*

**Dried apricots** *125 g (4¹/₂ oz), soaked in water for 2 hours, drained and finely diced (brunoise)*

**Chopped rosemary leaves** *2 tsp*

**Fine salt** *¹/₄ tsp*

**Ground black pepper** *¹/₈ tsp*

### CAPSICUMS

**Yellow capsicums (bell peppers)** *250 g (9 oz), cut in half and seeded*

**Red capsicums (bell peppers)** *250 g (9 oz), cut in half and seeded*

**Olive oil** *1 Tbsp*

**Fine salt** *¹/₈ tsp*

**Ground black pepper** *¹/₈ tsp*

### LAMB LOIN

**Boneless lamb loin** *600 g (1 lb 1¹/₂ oz), trimmed*

**Fine salt** *¹/₂ tsp*

**Ground black pepper** *¹/₄ tsp*

**Corn oil** *1 Tbsp*

**Lamb jus (see pg 170)** *60 ml (2 fl oz / 4 Tbsp)*

### GARNISH

**Rocket (arugula) leaves** *55 g (2 oz)*

Prepare apricot stuffing. Sauté shallots and garlic in olive oil. Add apricots and sauté for another few minutes. Transfer mixture to a bowl and allow to cool. When mixture is cool, add rosemary and season with salt and pepper. Spoon stuffing into a piping bag and set aside.

Place capsicum halves on a baking tray, skin side up and brush with olive oil. Season with salt and pepper and grill in the oven at 180°C (350°F) for about 15 minutes until skin is dark brown in colour. Remove from oven, peel off and discard skin. Cut grilled capsicums into thin square pieces. Set aside in a single layer on paper towels to remove excess liquid.

Pierce a hole through the centre of lamb loin with a knife. Pipe apricot stuffing into cavity. Season stuffed lamb with salt and pepper. Heat corn oil in a frying pan over high heat and sear lamb on all sides. Transfer lamb to a baking tray and cook in a preheated oven at 220°C (440°F) for 10 minutes. Remove from oven and let lamb rest for 5 minutes.

Slice lamb loin into 12 equal pieces. Serve with grilled capsicums and rocket leaves. Drizzle with warm lamb jus.

## Slow-Cooked Veal Fillet with Green Lentils

Start preparations 1 day ahead   Cooking Time: 2 hours 40 minutes   Serves 4

### LENTILS

**Green lentils** *200 g (7 oz), soaked for 12 hours*

**Water** *250 ml (8 fl oz / 1 cup)*

**Chicken stock (see pg 171)** *250 ml (8 fl oz / 1 cup)*

**Carrot** *55 g (1 1/2 oz), peeled and cut into chunks*

**Onion** *55 g (1 1/2 oz), peeled and cut into chunks*

**Celery** *55 g (1 1/2 oz), cut into chunks*

**Thyme** *1 sprig*

**Bay leaf** *1*

**Garlic** *2 cloves, peeled*

**Fine salt** *1/2 tsp*

**Ground black pepper** *1/4 tsp*

### LENTIL MIX

**Butter** *20 g (2/3 oz)*

**Carrot** *30 g (1 oz), peeled and finely diced*

**Celery** *30 g (1 oz), finely diced*

**Smoked streaky bacon** *55 g (2 oz), finely diced*

**Chervil** *10 g (1/3 oz), finely chopped*

### VEAL

**Veal fillet** *500 g (1 lb 1 1/2 oz), cleaned and trimmed*

**Chicken stock (see pg 171)** *100 ml (3 1/3 fl oz)*

**Thyme** *2 sprigs*

**Bay leaf** *1*

**Garlic** *1 clove, crushed*

**Butter** *1/2 Tbsp*

**Fine salt** *1/8 tsp*

**Ground black pepper** *1/8 tsp*

### GARNISH

**Leek** *200 g (7 oz)*

**Fine salt** *1/8 tsp*

**Ground black pepper** *1/8 tsp*

**Olive oil** *2 Tbsp*

**Black trumpet mushrooms (see Glossary)** *45 g (1 1/2 oz)*

Prepare lentils. Combine all ingredients for lentils in a pot and bring to a boil. Lower heat, cover and simmer for 1 hour 45 minutes. When lentils are tender, remove and discard all other vegetables and herbs. Drain lentils and set aside.

Prepare veal. Heat a pot of water to 70°C (155°F). Use a cooking thermometer to ensure temperature of water does not rise above 70°C (155°F) or veal will cook too fast and be tough. Place all ingredients for veal except salt, pepper and butter into a vacuum or food storage bag. Close and place bag on a steaming rack in pot. This ensures that the bag does not come in contact with the base of the pot. Alternatively, clip the bag to the side of the pot (see Kitchen Techniques). Veal takes 25–40 minutes to cook, depending on how well done you prefer the meat to be.

When veal is done, pour cooking juices from bag through a fine mesh sieve into a stainless steel pan. Reduce by half over medium-low heat and add butter to thicken. Season with salt and pepper. Set aside and keep warm.

Prepare garnish. Remove outer fibrous leaves of leek and cut tender middle part into long ribbons, about 12 cm x 1 cm (5 in x 1/2 in). Bring a pot of lightly salted water to a boil and blanch (see Note on pg 31) leek ribbons. Drain, reserving blanching liquid, and season blanched leek with salt, pepper and 1 tsp olive oil.

In the same liquid for blanching leek, warm trumpet mushrooms, then drain and set aside.

Prepare lentil mix just before serving. Heat butter in a pan and sauté finely diced carrot, celery and bacon until vegetables are translucent. Discard excess fat and add drained lentils. Mix well and sprinkle chervil over. Serve immediately with veal, leek, trumpet mushrooms and thickened juices. Drizzle remaining olive oil over.

# Vegetables and Tofu

Vegetables and tofu are always healthful food choices, with vegetables being an important part of a well-balanced diet, offering valuable nutrients and fibre, and tofu, a traditional soy product, being an excellent plant source of protein and iron. *Naturally Peninsula – Flavours* presents some great ideas for meatless dishes which will enthuse your taste buds with their wide range of interesting textures and terrific flavours. From baking to charring to steaming and blanching, from tofu sheets to silken tofu, from colourful root vegetables and their green leafy counterparts to vine-ripened tomatoes, hearts of palm and the prized black truffle, all of these elements come together to offer a tantalising variety of vegetable and tofu recipes.

## Vegetable Filo with Saffron Turmeric Sauce

Preparation Time: 1 hour   Cooking Time: 1 hour 30 minutes   Serves 4

**Filo pastry** *8 sheets, each 25 cm x 40 cm (10 in x 16 in)*

**Butter** *30 g (1 oz), softened*

### VEGETABLE FILLING

**Purple or white potato** *55 g (2 oz)*

**Red baby beetroot** *85 g (3 oz)*

**Fine salt** *¹/₈ tsp*

**Ground white pepper** *¹/₈ tsp*

**White asparagus** *30 g (1 oz), ends trimmed and peeled (see Kitchen Techniques)*

**Green asparagus** *30 g (1 oz), ends trimmed and peeled (see Kitchen Techniques)*

**Carrot** *55 g (2 oz), peeled and cut into 5 cm x 0.5 cm (2 in x ¹/₄ in) sticks*

**Spinach leaves** *30 g (1 oz)*

**Fennel bulb (see Glossary)** *30 g (1 oz), trimmed and cut into quarters*

**Garlic** *3 cloves, peeled and crushed*

**Butter** *30 g (1 oz)*

**Vegetable stock (see pg 170)** *300 ml (7 fl oz / ³/₄ cup)*

### TURMERIC SAUCE

**Olive oil** *2 tsp*

**Shallots** *4, peeled and chopped*

**Ground turmeric** *1 Tbsp*

**Red Thai bird's eye chilli (see Glossary)** *1, sliced, seeded and finely chopped*

**Vegetable stock (see pg 170)** *300 ml (10 fl oz / 1¹/₄ cups)*

**Saffron threads** *¹/₄ tsp*

**Single (light) cream** *60 ml (2 fl oz / 4 Tbsp)*

**Fine salt** *¹/₄ tsp*

**Ground black pepper** *¹/₈ tsp*

**Sugar** *³/₄ tsp*

### BEETROOT SAUCE

**Umeboshi plum** *15 g (¹/₂ oz)*

**Beetroot** *250 g (9 oz), peeled, put through a juicer and strained to extract 105 ml (3¹/₂ fl oz) juice*

**Olive oil** *¹/₂ Tbsp*

**NOTE**

Umeboshi plums are made by soaking unripened Japanese plums in brine. They are sometimes also packed with red shiso leaves for added flavour and a light red colouring. Puréed umeboshi is called *bainiku* and is often used as a seasoning. These salty and tart pickled plums can be found bottled or canned in Asian food markets.

Prepare filling. Bring a pot of lightly salted water to a boil and cook whole potato and baby beetroot until tender. Drain and cool. Peel potato and baby beetroot and cut into 5 cm x 0.5 cm (2 in x ¹/₄ in) sticks. Season with salt and pepper. Set aside.

Bring another pot of lightly salted water to a boil and blanch (see Note on pg 31) asparagus, carrot and spinach separately for 10 seconds each. Drain well and place on absorbent paper.

Place fennel, garlic, butter and vegetable stock in a pot and braise over low heat for 20 minutes or until fennel and garlic are soft. Strain and cool. The fennel should be of breakaway texture.

Divide vegetables into 4 portions. Lay a sheet of filo pastry on a work surface and brush lightly with butter. Place another sheet of filo on top and brush with butter again. Lay blanched spinach along the width of pastry then arrange remaining vegetables neatly on top. Roll into a cylinder and trim both ends. Repeat to make 4 rolls. Cut each roll in half and bake in a preheated oven at 200°C (400°F) for 20 minutes or until crisp and golden brown.

Prepare turmeric sauce. Heat oil and sauté shallots for 1–2 minutes over medium heat. Add turmeric, chilli and vegetable stock. Bring to a boil, then add saffron and reduce on low heat until a sauce-like consistency is achieved. Stir in cream and season with salt, pepper and sugar. Keep warm.

Prepare beetroot sauce. Remove flesh from plum and crush. Place in a pan with beetroot juice and cook over low heat, stirring, until reduced by half. Purée in a blender (food processor) and strain. Leave to cool before refrigerating until cold. When cold, gradually beat in olive oil. Keep refrigerated.

Serve filo rolls with turmeric sauce and beetroot sauce. Garnish as desired.

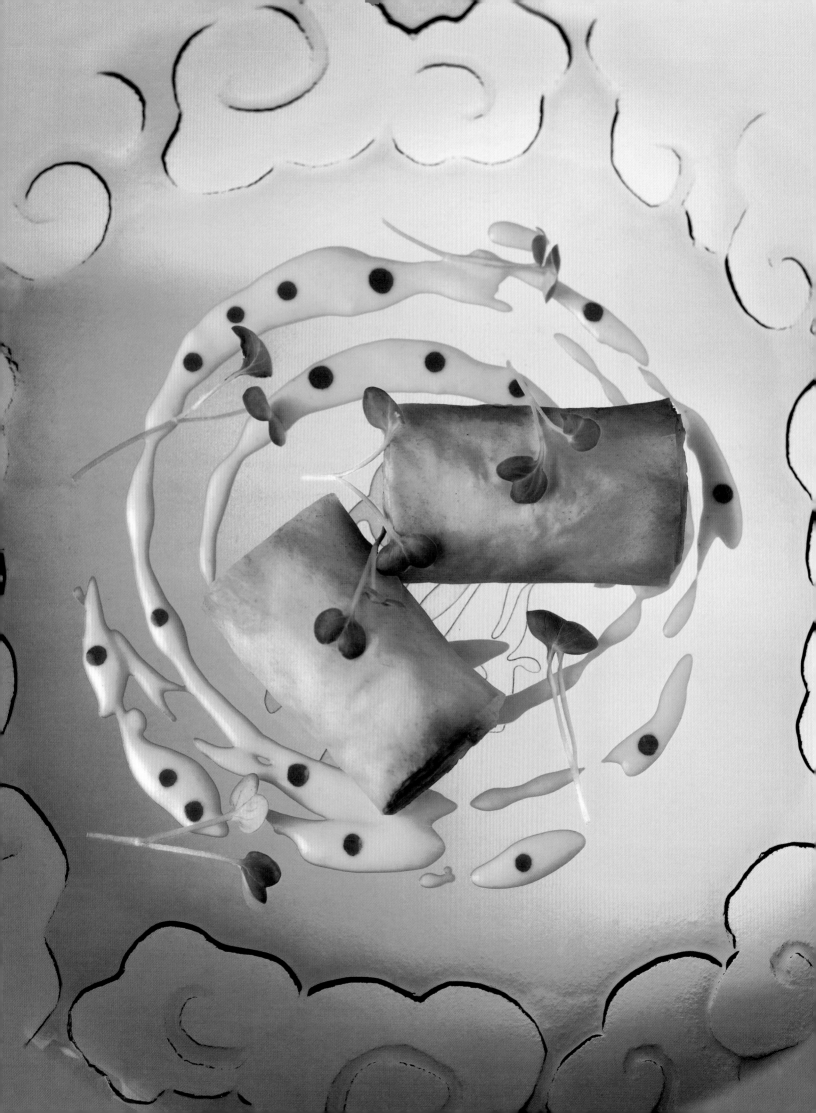

## Charred Hearts of Romaine with Fennel, Hearts of Palm and Orange-Ancho Vinaigrette

Preparation Time: 25 minutes   Cooking Time: 20 minutes   Serves 4

### ORANGE ANCHO VINAIGRETTE

Dried ancho chilli (see Glossary) *1*

Orange juice *500 ml (16 fl oz / 2 cups)*

Garlic *5 cloves, peeled*

Organic honey *2 Tbsp*

Rice wine vinegar *2 Tbsp*

Fine salt *1/8 tsp*

Ground black pepper *1/8 tsp*

### SALAD

Romaine hearts *4 equal size hearts, cut into quarters*

Fine salt *1/2 tsp*

Ground black pepper *1/4 tsp*

Oranges *4, peeled and cut into segments*

Fresh or canned hearts of palm *30 g (1 oz), sliced*

Fennel bulb (see Glossary) *115 g (3 1/2 oz), trimmed and cut into thin strips or shaved with a potato peeler*

**NOTE**
Hearts of palm refer to the edible ivory-coloured inner portions of the cabbage palm tree, with a firm, smooth texture and a delicate flavour similar to that of an artichoke. They are mostly used raw as a garnish in salads.

Prepare vinaigrette. Place dried chilli and orange juice in a pot and reduce over low heat to about 375 ml (12 fl oz / 1 1/2 cups). Takes about 15 minutes. Place reduction, along with garlic, honey and rice wine vinegar into a blender (food processor) and purée until smooth. Strain using a chinois or fine mesh sieve. Discard residue. Season vinaigrette with salt and pepper. Refrigerate to chill before serving.

Prepare salad. Season romaine hearts with salt and pepper. Place on a very hot grill for 10–15 seconds or until lightly charred. Discard limp outer leaves. Toss romaine hearts in a bowl with 3 Tbsp chilled vinaigrette. Drain.

Toss orange segments, hearts of palm, fennel and 125 ml (4 fl oz / 1/2 cup) vinaigrette in another mixing bowl. Drain.

Serve romaine hearts with orange segments, hearts of palm and fennel. Drizzle with remaining vinaigrette and garnish as desired.

*Photograph on pg 114–115*

## Pan-Fried Vegetable and Tofu Sheet Rolls

Preparation Time: 30 minutes   Cooking Time: 20 minutes   Serves 4

**Tofu sheets** 4, *cut into 20-cm (8-in) squares*

**Soy bean oil** *2 tsp*

**Celery** *85 g (3 oz), cut into 5-cm julienne strips*

**Enoki mushrooms** *70 g (2 1/2 oz), ends trimmed*

**Yam bean (jicama) (see Note on pg 40)**
*70 g (2 1/2 oz), cut into 5-cm (2 1/2-in) long julienne strips*

**Carrot** *70 g (2 1/2 oz) peeled and cut into 5-cm (2 1/2-in) long julienne strips*

**Light soy sauce** *1 Tbsp*

**Oyster sauce** *1 Tbsp*

**Sesame oil** *1/2 Tbsp*

**Plain (all-purpose) flour** *1 Tbsp*

**Egg white** *3 Tbsp*

**Soy bean or sunflower seed oil** *75 ml (2 1/2 fl oz / 5 Tbsp)*

**Umeboshi plums (see Note on pg 112)** *3, pressed through a sieve to purée*

**Water** *60 ml (2 fl oz / 4 Tbsp)*

**Rock sugar** *100 g (3 1/2 oz)*

**Sugar** *100 g (3 1/2 oz)*

**Red chilli** *1, seeded and cut into 0.3-cm (1/8-in) dice*

**Pickled ginger** *15 g (1/2 oz / 1 Tbsp), cut into fine julienne*

**Rice vinegar** *2 Tbsp*

Wipe tofu sheets with a damp cloth to remove excess salt. Set aside.

Heat soy bean oil and sauté celery, mushrooms, yam bean and carrot over medium-high heat. Season to taste with light soy sauce, oyster sauce and sesame oil. Leave to cool.

Mix flour and egg white well together. Set aside.

Place a tofu sheet on a work surface, with a corner pointing towards you. Spoon about 45 g (1 1/2 oz) sautéed vegetables onto the portion of tofu sheet nearest you. Fold the corner nearest you over filling, then fold the left and right hand corners over and roll up into a log. Seal with some flour and egg white mixture. Repeat to make 4 rolls.

Heat oil to about 170°C (330°F) and pan-fry rolls until golden brown and crispy. Drain and leave to cool. Reheat oil and refry rolls just before serving for an extra crisp skin.

Prepare plum sauce. Combine all ingredients except vinegar in a pot. Bring to a boil, then lower heat and simmer over low heat for 5–7 minutes or until mixture is just starting to become syrupy. Stir in rice vinegar and remove from heat.

Serve rolls hot with plum sauce.

*Photograph on pg 118–119*

# Savoury Tart of Vine-Ripened Tomatoes with Young Spinach and Basil Sherbet

Start preparations 1½ days ahead   Cooking Time: 1 hour   Serves 4

### BASIL SHERBET

Basil leaves *75 g (2½ oz)*

Plain yoghurt *75 g (2½ oz)*

Sugar syrup *75 ml (2½ fl oz / 5 Tbsp)*

### OVEN-DRIED TOMATOES

Vine-ripened plum (Roma) tomatoes *750 g (1 lb 11 oz)*

Fine salt *½ tsp*

Ground black pepper *¼ tsp*

Sugar *1 tsp*

Garlic *2 cloves, peeled and thinly sliced*

Chopped basil leaves *1 Tbsp*

Chopped rosemary leaves *1 Tbsp*

Chopped thyme leaves *1 Tbsp*

Olive oil *105 ml (3½ fl oz)*

### OLIVE TAPENADE

Black pitted olives *70 g (2½ oz)*

Olive oil *105 ml (3½ fl oz)*

### FILO DISCS

Filo sheets *2, each 40 cm x 25 cm (16 in x 10-in)*

Egg yolk *1*

Olive oil *1 Tbsp*

### GARNISH

Cherry tomatoes

Basil leaves

**NOTE**
Make a simple sugar syrup by bringing equal parts of sugar and water to a boil and simmering until the sugar dissolves and the syrup is clear. Cool to room temperature before using.

Prepare basil sherbet. Bring a pot of lightly salted water to a boil and blanch (see Note on pg 31) basil leaves for 5 seconds. Drain and place into an ice bath immediately. Drain. Blend (process) basil leaves with yoghurt and syrup, then churn in an ice cream maker according to the manufacturer's instructions. Freeze until ready to serve.

Prepare oven-dried tomatoes. Using a small sharp knife, mark an 'X' on each tomato (see Note on pg 39). Bring a pot of lightly salted water to a boil. Blanch tomatoes for 20 seconds, then peel and discard skin. Cut tomatoes into quarters and remove soft centres. Place on a baking tray and season with salt, pepper and sugar. Sprinkle remaining ingredients over and dry in a preheated oven at 65°C (150°F) for 1 hour.

Prepare olive tapenade. Place olives and olive oil in a blender (food processor) and purée. Set aside.

Prepare filo discs. Using an 11-cm (4½-in) round cutter, cut out 6 rounds from each filo sheet. Brush edges of pastry rounds with egg yolk and stack 3 rounds on top of each other to get a total of 4 filo discs. Brush filo discs with olive oil and place in a preheated oven at 220°C (420°F) for 1–2 minutes until golden brown and crisp.

Spread olive tapenade on top of each filo disc and top with oven-dried tomatoes and basil sherbet. Drizzle with more olive tapenade and garnish with cherry tomatoes and basil leaves. Serve immediately.

## Steamed Tofu with Asparagus and Black Fungus

Preparation Time: 20 minutes   Cooking Time: 30 minutes   Serves 4

### STEAMED TOFU

**Silken tofu** *600 g (1 lb 5¹/₃ oz)*

**Asparagus** *100 g (3¹/₂ oz), peeled and trimmed (see Kitchen Techniques)*

**Black fungus (see Glossary)** *70 g (2¹/₂ oz), weighed after soaking, trimmed of hard portions*

**Chinese wolfberries (see Glossary)** *15 g (¹/₂ oz)*

### SAUCE

**Chicken stock (see pg 171)** *1 litre (32 fl oz / 4 cups)*

**Dark soy sauce** *1 tsp*

**Light soy sauce** *1 tsp*

**Corn flour (cornstarch)** *1 Tbsp, mixed with 1 Tbsp water*

**Sesame oil** *¹/₄ tsp*

**Fine salt** *¹/₄ tsp*

**Ground white pepper** *¹/₄ tsp*

Prepare steamed tofu. Using a 4-cm (1¹/₂-in) round cutter, cut tofu into 12 rounds, each about 1-cm (¹/₂-in) thick. Alternatively, purchase tofu packaged in a tube and cut into 1-cm (¹/₂-in) thick slices. Set aside.

Bring a pot of lightly salted water to a boil and blanch asparagus for 1 minute. Refresh in ice water and drain. Set aside.

Place black fungus, wolfberries and tofu rounds separately on a steaming plate. Steam for 2 minutes.

Prepare sauce. Bring chicken stock to a boil, then lower to medium heat and allow stock to reduce by half. Add dark and light soy sauces, then stir in corn flour mixture to thicken sauce. Return to a boil and add sesame oil just before removing from heat. Season with salt and pepper.

Serve tofu rounds with asparagus, black fungus and Chinese wolfberries in sauce.

## Root Vegetable Pot-Au-Feu with Madeira and Black Truffle Broth

Preparation Time: 45 minutes   Cooking Time: 1 hour   Serves 4

**Thyme** *1 sprig*

**Bay leaf** *1*

**Garlic** *1 clove, peeled and crushed*

**Madeira wine** *75 ml (2¹/₂ fl oz / 5 Tbsp)*

**Vegetable stock (see pg 170)** *625 ml (20 fl oz / 2¹/₂ cups)*

**Baby turnips** *100 g (3¹/₂ oz), peeled*

**Celeriac root (see Glossary)** *200 g (7 oz), peeled and cut into 4 cm x 1 cm (1¹/₂ in x ¹/₂ in) sticks*

**Celery** *150 g (5¹/₃ oz), peeled and cut into 4 cm x 1 cm (1¹/₂ in x ¹/₂ in) sticks*

**Red radish** *100 g (3¹/₂ oz), cut into bite-size pieces*

**Baby leeks** *12*

**Black Périgord truffle (see Glossary)** *85 g (3 oz), thinly sliced*

**Fine salt** *¹/₂ tsp*

**Ground black pepper** *¹/₂ tsp*

**Celery leaves** *12, cleaned*

**NOTE**
See Note on pg 100 on pot-au-feu.

Place thyme, bay leaf, garlic, wine and vegetable stock in an ovenproof pot and bring to a boil. Add turnips, celeriac, celery, radish, leeks and truffle and cover with a tight-fitting lid.

Place pot in a preheated oven at 90°C (195°F) and cook for 45 minutes or until vegetables are tender. Season with salt and pepper.

Garnish with celery leaves and serve immediately.

## Saffron-Infused Kohlrabi Tiles with Grilled Vegetables and Truffle Coulis

Preparation Time: 30 minutes   Cooking Time: 1 hour   Serves 4

### SAFFRON-INFUSED KOHLRABI

Kohlrabi (see Glossary) *800 g (1³/₄ lb)*

Saffron threads *¹/₈ tsp*

Fine salt *1 tsp*

Ground black pepper *¹/₄ tsp*

Water *1 litre (32 fl oz / 4 cups)*

### GRILLED VEGETABLES

Leeks *2 stalks, ends trimmed and cut into 4 sticks, each 15 cm x 1 cm (6 in x ¹/₂ in)*

Fine salt *¹/₈ tsp*

Ground black pepper *¹/₈ tsp*

Baby Belgium endives *4, each cut in half*

Pumpkin flesh *160 g (5¹/₂ oz)*

Coarsely ground black pepper *¹/₂ tsp*

Black truffle oil *60 ml (2 fl oz / 4 Tbsp)*

### TRUFFLE COULIS

Black truffle oil *60 ml (2 fl oz / 4 Tbsp)*

Black Périgord truffle (see Glossary) *55 g (2 oz), chopped*

Plain yoghurt *2 Tbsp*

Fine salt *¹/₈ tsp*

Ground black pepper *¹/₈ tsp*

### GARNISH

Fleur de Sel de Guérande *¹/₄ tsp*

Sarawak pepper *¹/₄ tsp, crushed*

### NOTE

Fleur de Sel de Guérande is a premium sea salt harvested by hand from the salt marshes of Guérande off the coast of France. With its creamy-white granules that are exquisitely delicate and moist, it is considered one of the richest and most flavourful salts and is not usually used for cooking but as a condiment to be sprinkled over the finished dish.

Sarawak pepper is cultivated in Sarawak, Malaysia. It is known for its bold flavour and taste.

A coulis is a thick sauce made from puréed (and sometimes strained) vegetables or fruit. Vegetable coulis is a common sauce for meat and vegetable dishes, and it can also be used as a base for soups or other sauces. Fruit coulis is most often used with desserts.

Prepare saffron-infused kohlrabi. Peel and cut kohlrabi into 1.5 cm x 1.5 cm x 0.5 cm (³/₄ in x ³/₄ in x ¹/₄ in) squares. Place trimmings into a pot with saffron, salt, pepper and water to make a stock. Bring to a boil and simmer mixture over low heat for 30 minutes. Strain stock and return to the pot. Discard trimmings. Place kohlrabi squares into the pot and bring to a boil, cooking until kohlrabi is soft. Carefully remove from stock and place on a plate. Cover with plastic wrap (cling film) and refrigerate.

Bring a pot of lightly salted water to a boil and blanch (see Note on pg 31) leeks. Drain, pat dry and season with salt and pepper. Grill leeks and endives over charcoal until grill marks form on vegetables. Alternatively, cook over the stovetop using a grill pan to create brown grill marks on vegetables.

Cut pumpkin into wedges. Sprinkle pumpkin with coarsely ground black pepper. Heat truffle oil in a grill pan over medium heat and cook pumpkin.

Prepare truffle coulis. Heat truffle oil over medium heat and add chopped truffle. Cook, stirring until truffle is very soft. Place truffle in a blender (food processor) and purée until smooth. Remove paste and mix well with yoghurt. Season with salt and pepper.

Serve kohlrabi tiles with leek, endive, pumpkin and truffle coulis. Finish with Fleur de Sel de Guérande and crushed Sarawak pepper.

# Rice and Pasta

It's back to the basics in this chapter where beautiful home-made pastas feature in three different forms — lasagne, ravioli and tortellini — supported by a splendid array of fresh herbs and vegetables in three colourful and appetising recipes. A pasta machine helps but a good rolling pin, strong arms and an even stronger determination will result in lovely thin sheets of pasta which will rival the best that is on offer. Other innovative recipes include using Italian risotto rice to create a Japanese-inspired asparagus sushi roll with a crispy twist, and a simple but delicious mushroom risotto made with wholesome organic brown rice. *Naturally Peninsula – Flavours* provides interesting interpretations of everyday ingredients, often presenting fresh new treatments that transform the ordinary into the extraordinary!

## Butternut Pumpkin Risotto with Pancetta and Toasted Pecan Mascarpone

Preparation Time: 25 minutes   Cooking Time: 35 minutes   Serves 4

### TOASTED PECAN MASCARPONE

**Pecans** 30 g (1 oz), cut in half

**Mascarpone cheese** 55 g (2 oz)

### RAGOUT

**Canola oil** 1 Tbsp

**Pancetta** 85 g (3 oz), diced

**Butternut pumpkin flesh** 85 g (3 oz), diced

**Brussels sprouts** 55 g (2 oz), cut into quarters

**Fine salt** 1/2 tsp

**Ground black pepper** 1/4 tsp

### RISOTTO

**Onion** 45 g (1 1/2 oz), peeled and diced

**Butter** 45 g (1 1/2 oz)

**Arborio rice** 210 g (7 1/3 oz), washed and drained

**Dry white wine** 125 ml (4 fl oz / 1/2 cup)

**Chicken stock (see pg 171)** 625 ml (20 fl oz / 2 1/2 cups), kept hot

**Grated Parmesan cheese** 45 g (1 1/2 oz)

**Fine salt** 3/8 tsp

**Coarsely ground black pepper** 1/8 tsp

**NOTE**
Pancetta is an Italian bacon made from belly pork. It is dry-cured (but not smoked) with salt, pepper and spices, then rolled up and bound.

Prepare toasted pecan mascarpone. Lay pecans out on a baking tray and bake in a preheated oven at 180°C (350°F) for 5 minutes. Allow to cool, then chop coarsely. Beat mascarpone lightly with a fork to fluff up cheese. Fold toasted pecans into mascarpone and set aside.

Prepare ragout. Heat oil in a pan over medium-low heat. Add pancetta and cook slowly for about 4 minutes over medium heat until meat is well-caramelised. Add butternut pumpkin and continue to cook for 2–3 minutes until pumpkin is soft.

Bring a pot of lightly salted water to a boil and blanch (see Note on pg 31) Brussels sprouts for 1 minute. Drain and add to pan with pancetta and pumpkin. Season with salt and pepper. Set aside in a warm place.

Prepare risotto. Sweat (see Note on pg 20) onion in half the butter over medium heat for 2–3 minutes. Add rice and mix thoroughly. Pour in wine and stir until liquid is absorbed. Add one-third of stock and stir until stock is absorbed. Repeat with remaining stock in 4 separate additions. Cook until rice is al dente (see Note on pg 68) and most of liquid is absorbed.

Stir mascarpone and ragout mixture into rice. Fold in remaining butter and Parmesan. Season with salt and pepper. Garnish as desired and serve immediately.

## Organic Vegetable Lasagne with Thai Rosella

Preparation Time: 1 hour 45 minutes   Cooking Time: 1 hour   Serves 4

### PURPLE PASTA

**Beetroot** 280 g (10 oz), peeled, put through a juicer and strained to extract 150 ml (5 fl oz / 10 Tbsp) juice

**Purified water**

**Egg yolk** 1

**Organic extra virgin olive oil** 2 tsp

**Sea salt** $^1/_3$ tsp

**Organic flour** 150 g (5$^1/_2$ oz)

### GREEN PASTA

**Parsley leaves** 100 g (3$^1/_2$ oz)

**Purified water** 500 ml (16 fl oz / 2 cups) + 30–60 ml (1–2 fl oz / 2–4 Tbsp)

**Egg yolk** 1

**Extra virgin olive oil** 2 tsp

**Sea salt** $^1/_3$ tsp

**Organic flour** 150 g (5$^1/_2$ oz)

### PLAIN PASTA

**Purified water** 70 ml (2$^1/_3$ fl oz)

**Egg yolk** 1

**Extra virgin olive oil** 2 tsp

**Sea salt** $^1/_3$ tsp

**Organic flour** 150 g (5$^1/_2$ oz)

### EGG WASH

**Egg** 1, beaten

### QUINOA

**Organic white quinoa (see Glossary)** 140 g (5 oz)

**Water** 1 litre (32 fl oz / 4 cups), mixed with 1 tsp fine salt

### ORGANIC VEGETABLES

**Organic Thai green asparagus** 70 g (2$^1/_2$ oz), peeled, trimmed and cut into even-size pieces (see Kitchen Techniques)

**Organic baby carrots** 70 g (2$^1/_2$ oz), cut into even-size pieces

**Organic beetroot** 70 g (2$^1/_2$ oz), peeled and cut into even-size pieces

**Organic baby bok choy** 70 g (2$^1/_2$ oz)

**Fine salt** $^1/_4$ tsp

**Ground black pepper** $^1/_8$ tsp

### SICHUAN ORANGE SAUCE

**Orange juice** 300 ml (10 fl oz / 1$^1/_4$ cups)

**Sichuan peppercorns** 2 tsp

### THAI ROSELLA

**Rose water** 1 tsp

**Purified water** 125 ml (4 fl oz / $^1/_2$ cup)

**Dried Thai rosella (see Glossary)** 4

### NOTE

Flour varies in absorbency levels, so if you find that the pasta dough is too hard and flaky, add water, a few drops at a time, until the pasta dough is pliable. If the pasta dough is too wet, sprinkle a little more flour and knead it in until the dough is pliable.

Sichuan peppercorns are not related to the peppercorn family but are actually dried berries from the prickly ash tree which contain a tiny seed. It is a mildly hot spice with a distinctive flavour and aroma.

Rose water is a by-product of the steam distillation of rose petals (to extract its essential oils) and has a perfumy sweetness and delicate flavour.

Prepare tri-coloured pasta (see Kitchen Techniques).

For purple pasta, reduce beetroot juice in pot over low heat by two-thirds. Strain through a chinois or fine mesh sieve and leave to cool. There should be about 50 ml (1$^2/_3$ fl oz) thickened beetroot juice. Add enough purified water to make up 70 ml (2$^1/_3$ fl oz). Combine beetroot juice, egg yolk, olive oil and sea salt. Pour into a mixing bowl with flour. Using a cake mixer with a dough hook, knead to achieve smooth dough. Cover dough with plastic wrap (cling film) and leave to rest for 1 hour.

For green pasta, blend (process) parsley leaves with water until water turns green. Strain through a chinois or a fine mesh sieve into a pot. Discard residue. Bring parsley juice to just below boiling and skim off any green substance that forms on the surface of water. This green substance is chlorophyll from the parsley leaves. Place chlorophyll into a small cup and cool immediately by half immersing cup in an ice water bath to keep the colour brilliant. Add enough additional water to chlorophyll to obtain 70 ml (2$^1/_3$ fl oz) liquid. Combine chlorophyll, egg yolk, olive oil and sea salt. Pour into a mixing bowl with flour. Using a cake mixer with a dough hook, knead to achieve smooth dough. Cover dough with plastic wrap (cling film) and leave to rest for 1 hour.

For plain pasta, mix water with egg yolk, olive oil and salt. Pour into a mixing bowl with flour. Using a cake mixer with a dough hook, knead to achieve smooth dough. Cover dough with plastic wrap (cling film) and leave to rest for 1 hour.

Roll out all 3 types of pasta dough very thinly with a rolling pin or pasta machine. Cut thin strips out of beetroot and parsley dough. Cut plain dough into 5-cm (2-in) squares. Lay plain dough squares on a work surface and brush with egg wash. Line with beetroot and parsley pasta to form striped pasta. Roll out using a rolling pin or pasta machine to combine pasta. Trim edges to obtain 5-cm (2-in) squares.

Wash quinoa under cold running water before cooking in boiling lightly salted water for 15 minutes. Strain and cool. Sauté over high heat just before serving.

Prepare Sichuan orange sauce. Pour orange juice into a pot and add peppercorns. Reduce over low heat to a thick sauce. Set aside.

Steam vegetables for 3 minutes. Sprinkle with salt and pepper and set aside.

Prepare Thai rosella. Combine rose water and purified water in a pot and bring to a boil. Place rosella in and cook until soft. Drain.

Just before serving, blanch fresh pasta squares in salted boiling water for 1 minute and drain. Serve pasta with quinoa, vegetables and rosella. Drizzle with Sichuan orange sauce. Garnish as desired.

## Organic Long-Grain Brown Rice Risotto with Mushrooms

Preparation Time: 40 minutes   Cooking Time: 35 minutes   Serves 4 as a main course and 6 as an appetiser

### RISOTTO

**Onions** 45 g (1¹/₂ oz), peeled and chopped

**Fresh shiitake mushrooms** 125 g (4¹/₂ oz), sliced

**Dried morels (see Glossary)** 10 g (¹/₃ oz), soaked in 300 ml (10 fl oz / 1¹/₄ cups) water to soften, then sliced; reserve soaking liquid

**Olive oil** 3 Tbsp

**Organic long-grain brown rice** 240 g (8¹/₂ oz), washed and drained

**Vegetable stock (see pg 170)** 625–900 ml (20–28 fl oz / 3–4 cups)

### GARNISH

**Rocket (arugula) leaves** 30 g (1 oz)

**Porcini (cep) (see Glossary)** 30 g (1 oz), grilled and sliced

**White button mushrooms** 85 g (3 oz), left raw and sliced

**Extra virgin olive oil** 4 tsp

**NOTE**
This dish tastes delicious without adding extra salt, as there is already salt present in the vegetable stock.

Sauté onions, shiitake and morels in olive oil for 2–3 minutes. Add rice and sauté for a few seconds, mixing ingredients well. Slowly add 100 ml (3 fl oz / ³/₈ cup) vegetable stock and about 250 ml (8 fl oz / 1 cup) morel soaking liquid and simmer until stock is absorbed.

Add another 100 ml (3 fl oz / ³/₈ cup) vegetable stock and simmer. Repeat until rice is fully cooked, but still has a little bite. Takes about 20 minutes.

Serve risotto garnished with rocket leaves and mushrooms. Drizzle with olive oil and serve immediately.

## Seven Vegetable Ravioli with Broad Bean Purée and Sweet Corn Emulsion

Preparation Time: 1 hour   Cooking Time: 30 minutes   Serves 4

### RAVIOLI

Bread flour *250 g (9 oz)*

Eggs *3, medium-size*

Olive oil *2 Tbsp*

Egg yolk *1, beaten*

Butter *30 g (1 oz)*

### RAVIOLI FILLING

Butter *30 g (1 oz)*

Shallots *30 g (1 oz), peeled and finely sliced*

Spinach *320 g (11 oz), stems discarded, leaves roughly chopped*

Mascarpone *55 g (2 oz)*

Fine salt *¹/₄ tsp or to taste*

Ground black pepper *¹/₄ tsp*

### VEGETABLES

Carrots *85 g (3 oz), peeled and cut into even-size pieces*

Courgette (zucchini) *85 g (3 oz), peeled and cut into even-size pieces*

Asparagus *85 g (3 oz), peeled, trimmed and cut into even-size pieces (see Kitchen Techniques)*

Red radish *85 g (3 oz), cut into even-size pieces*

Broccoli *85 g (3 oz), cut into small florets*

Chanterelles (see Glossary) *85 g (3 oz)*

Butter *30 g (1 oz)*

Fine salt *¹/₄ tsp*

Ground black pepper *¹/₄ tsp*

### BROAD BEAN PURÉE

Vegetable stock (see pg 170) *200 ml (6²/₃ fl oz)*

Broad (fava) beans (see Glossary) *180 g (6 oz)*

Whipping cream *60 ml (2 fl oz / 4 Tbsp)*

Fine salt *¹/₄ tsp*

Ground black pepper *¹/₈ tsp*

### SWEET CORN EMULSION

Butter *30 g (1 oz)*

Sweet corn kernels *125 g (4¹/₂ oz)*

Vegetable stock (see pg 170) *90 ml (3 fl oz)*

Fine salt *¹/₈ tsp*

Ground black pepper *¹/₈ tsp*

Prepare ravioli. Combine flour, eggs and olive oil using a cake mixer with a dough hook to form smooth dough. Add more flour if dough is sticky. Wrap dough in plastic wrap (cling film) and leave to rest for 30 minutes. Divide dough into 2 equal parts and roll out into thin sheets using a rolling pin or pasta machine. Trim so they are of equal size. Set aside.

Prepare ravioli filling. Heat butter and sauté shallots over medium heat for 1 minute. Add spinach leaves and mascarpone and sauté for another 1 minute on medium-high heat. Season with salt and pepper.

To make ravioli, lay a sheet of pasta dough on a work surface. Spoon mounds of filling, about 30 g (1 oz) each, on sheet, leaving enough space between mounds for rim of ravioli. Brush egg yolk around filling and lay other sheet of pasta over, ensuring the 2 sheets match up evenly. Using your fingers, gently ease out any air bubbles from edge of filling so raviolis will not explode due to the expansion of trapped air when cooking. Using a round cookie cutter, cut out ravioli. Ensure edges are tightly sealed.

Bring a pot of lightly salted water to a boil and lower ravioli in to cook. Takes 4–5 minutes. Drain and set aside. Just before serving, heat butter in a pan and sauté ravioli over medium heat. Serve immediately.

Prepare vegetables. Bring a pot of lightly salted water to a boil and blanch (see Note on pg 31) vegetables and mushrooms separately to half-cook them. Drain well. Heat butter in a pan and sauté vegetables and mushrooms over medium heat. Season with salt and pepper. Set aside.

Prepare broad bean purée. Heat vegetable stock and blanch beans over medium-high heat for 1¹/₂ minutes. Place in a blender (food processor) and add whipping cream. Blend (process) into a smooth purée. Season with salt and pepper. Set aside.

Prepare sweet corn emulsion. Heat butter in a pan and sauté corn kernels over medium-low heat for 2 minutes. Add vegetable stock and simmer for 3 minutes. Place in a blender (food processor) and purée while warm at high speed until very fine. Season with salt and pepper.

Serve ravioli with broad bean purée, sautéed vegetables and mushrooms and sweet corn emulsion. Garnish as desired.

## Crispy Asparagus and Organic Saffron Rice Roll with Nori and Wasabi Yoghurt

Preparation Time: 30 minutes   Cooking Time: 40 minutes   Serves 4

**Asparagus** *125 g (4¹/₂ oz), peeled and trimmed (see Kitchen Techniques)*

RICE ROLL

**Olive oil** *2 tsp*

**Shallots** *45 g (1¹/₂ oz), peeled and chopped*

**Organic Arborio rice** *170 g (6 oz), washed and drained*

**Saffron threads** *¹/₄ tsp*

**Chicken stock (see pg 171)** *500 ml (16 fl oz / 2 cups), kept warm*

**Fine salt** *¹/₂ tsp*

**Ground white pepper** *¹/₄ tsp*

**Nori (Japanese seaweed)** *4 sheets*

**Corn flour (cornstarch)** *2 tsp, mixed with 1 Tbsp water*

**Japanese breadcrumbs (panko)** *45 g (1¹/₂ oz)*

**Canola oil** *90 ml (3 fl oz / 6 Tbsp)*

WASABI YOGHURT

**Plain yoghurt** *80 g (2¹/₂ fl oz / ¹/₃ cup)*

**Wasabi powder** *2 tsp*

Bring a pot of lightly salted water to a boil and blanch (see Note on pg 31) asparagus for 2 minutes. Refresh in ice water, drain and pat dry. Set aside.

In a saucepan, heat olive oil over medium-low heat. Add shallots and sweat (see Note on pg 20) for 2 minutes. Add rice and saffron and stir-fry for a few seconds before gradually adding chicken stock in 2 batches. Cook, stirring until stock is absorbed before adding next portion of chicken stock. Takes about 25 minutes. Season with salt and pepper. Stir to mix well and set aside.

Lay a nori sheet on a bamboo mat made for rolling sushi. Spoon risotto along one length of nori and place 3 asparagus spears on top. Roll up tightly "sushi style" to enclose asparagus. Repeat to make 4 rolls. Brush rolls with corn flour mixture and roll in breadcrumbs.

Heat oil and fry rice rolls until golden brown on all sides. Drain on absorbent paper.

Mix yoghurt with wasabi powder.

Cut each rice roll into 4 equal slices and serve with wasabi yoghurt. Garnish as desired.

# Herb Purée Tortellini with Parmesan and Garlic Cream Cappuccino

Start preparations 3 hours ahead   Cooking Time: 1 hour   Serves 4

### PASTA DOUGH

Saffron threads *¹/₈ tsp*

Fine salt *³/₄ tsp*

Warm water *90 ml (3 fl oz / 6 Tbsp)*

Olive oil *2 Tbsp*

Egg *1*

Egg yolks *4*

Plain (all-purpose) flour *300 g (10 oz)*

### TORTELLINI FILLING

Butter *30 g (1 oz)*

Shallots *5, peeled and cut into 1-cm (¹/₂-in) cubes*

Spinach *255 g (9 oz), stems discarded*

Fine salt *¹/₈ tsp*

Ground black pepper *¹/₈ tsp*

Double (heavy) cream *2 Tbsp, strained*

Garlic *1 clove, peeled and chopped*

Parmesan cheese *45 g (1¹/₂ oz), grated*

Mascarpone *30 g (1 oz)*

Chives *10 g (¹/₃ oz), finely sliced*

Chervil *10 g (¹/₃ oz), finely sliced*

Parsley *10 g (¹/₃ oz), finely sliced*

### TORTELLINI

Egg yolk *1, beaten*

Olive oil *1 tsp*

### GARLIC CREAM CAPPUCCINO

Butter *105 g (3¹/₂ oz)*

Shallots *30 g (1 oz), peeled and finely chopped*

Garlic *2 cloves, peeled and finely chopped*

Thyme *2 sprigs*

Bay leaf *1*

White wine *105 ml (3¹/₂ fl oz)*

Chicken stock (see pg 171) *195 ml (6¹/₂ fl oz)*

Double (heavy) cream *105 ml (3¹/₂ fl oz)*

Salt *³/₄ tsp*

Ground white pepper *¹/₄ tsp*

Prepare pasta dough. Add saffron and salt to warm water. Stir to dissolve salt and allow saffron to infuse. Add olive oil, egg and egg yolks. Whisk thoroughly and pass through a fine mesh sieve. Place flour into a mixing bowl. Using a cake mixer with a dough hook, gradually add egg mixture to flour and mix until a firm dough is formed. Wrap dough in plastic wrap (cling film) and leave to rest for 1 hour. Divide dough into 4 equal portions and keep covered until needed.

Prepare tortellini filling. Heat butter and sweat shallots over medium heat until translucent. Add spinach leaves and sauté quickly over high heat. Season with salt and pepper. Leave spinach to cool, then squeeze out any excess liquid. Chop finely and place in a pot with remaining ingredients. Refrigerate for 1–2 hours until firm.

To make tortellini, divide filling into small balls, about 10 g (¹/₃ oz) each. You should get about 28 balls.

Roll pasta dough with a rolling pin or pasta machine into 0.2-cm (¹/₁₀-in) thick sheets. Cut out 28 squares, each 5-cm (2-in) and place on a tray. Place a ball of filling onto the centre of each square. Brush egg yolk on half of each square and bring 2 opposite sides together to seal. Just before serving, bring a pot of lightly salted water to a boil and add olive oil. Lower tortellini in to cook for 4–5 minutes. Drain.

Prepare garlic cream cappuccino (see Kitchen Techniques). Heat one-third of butter in a pan and sauté shallots, garlic, thyme and bay leaf until shallots are translucent. Add white wine and bring to a boil. Add chicken stock and cream and reduce by half over medium-low heat. Remove and discard thyme and bay leaf. Pour mixture into a blender (food processor) and purée until smooth. Strain through a fine mesh sieve. Season with salt and pepper. Just before serving, whisk in remaining butter until sauce is foamy.

Serve tortellini topped with garlic cream cappuccino. Garnish as desired.

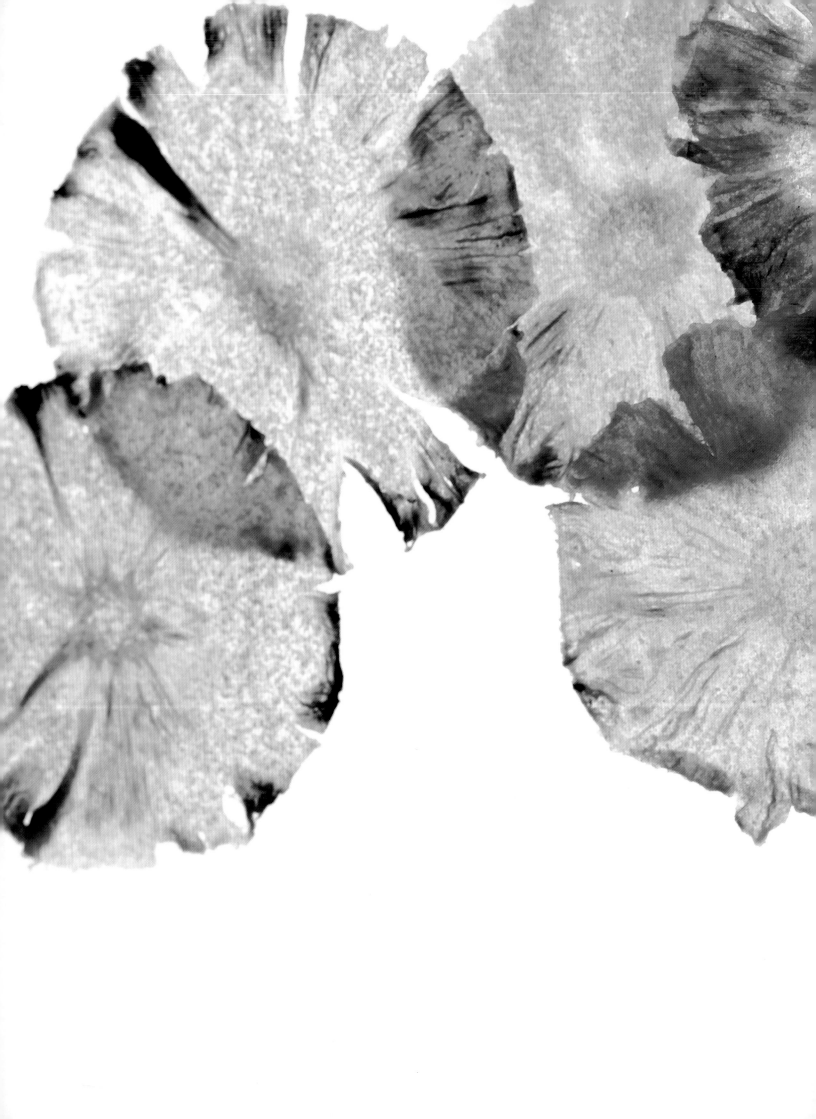

# Desserts

A delicious dessert should be the crowning finale to every meal, the perfect conclusion to all memorable dining occasions. Dessert is definitely not treated as merely an afterthought in *Naturally Peninsula – Flavours*, where unique combinations of fruit, cakes, sorbets and dessert sauces offer a whole new slant to the traditional sweet endings of a meal. From a refreshing dessert soup served with frozen yoghurt to roasted tropical fruit cooked with chilli and drizzled with beetroot jus; from chocolate cupcakes with a soy milk chocolate frosting and sauce to a delightful fruit consommé made with plump summer berries, and a tropical-style napoleon accompanied by a vanilla-tapioca sauce, these are just a few of the delectable dessert selections that are guaranteed to end your meal on a high note.

## Brown Sugar Angel Food Cakes with Passion Fruit Sorbet and Vanilla-Marinated Fruit

Start preparations 1¹/₂ days ahead   Cooking Time: 30 minutes   Serves 4

### ANGEL FOOD CAKES

Plain (all-purpose) flour *100 g (3¹/₂ oz)*

Light brown sugar *150 g (5¹/₃ oz)*

Egg whites *300 g (11 oz)*

Cream of tartar *¹/₂ Tbsp*

Castor (superfine) sugar *100 g (3¹/₂ oz)*

Fine salt *¹/₂ tsp*

Vanilla essence *1¹/₂ tsp*

Lemon juice *1¹/₂ tsp*

Lemons *2, grated for zest*

Icing (confectioners') sugar *for dusting*

### PASSION FRUIT SORBET

Water *180 ml (6 fl oz)*

Castor (superfine) sugar *150 g (5¹/₃ oz)*

Glucose *70 g (2¹/₂ oz)*

Stabilizer (gelatine powder) *5 g (1 tsp)*

Passion fruit purée *500 g (1 lb 1¹/₂ oz)*

### VANILLA-MARINATED FRUIT

Vanilla bean *1*

Organic honey *60 ml (2 fl oz / 4 Tbsp)*

Raspberries *200 g (7 oz)*

Blueberries *200 g (7 oz)*

Strawberries *200 g (7 oz), hulled and quartered*

Plum *1, cut into thin wedges*

**NOTE**

Passion fruit purée is available from baking supplies stores. To make your own purée, use 16 passion fruit weighing an average of 55 g (2 oz) each. Extract the pulp from the fruit and blend (process) at high speed together with the seeds. Makes about 500 g (1 lb 1¹/₂ oz) purée.

Prepare angel food cakes. Preheat oven to 170°C (330°F). Sift flour and brown sugar together 3 times and set aside. Whip egg whites until frothy, then add cream of tartar and beat until soft peaks form. Slowly add castor sugar and salt and beat until stiff shiny peaks form. Fold flour mixture into meringue just until combined. Fold vanilla essence, lemon juice and zest into batter and incorporate well.

Spoon batter into non-stick baking cups 8.5 cm (3¹/₂ in) in diameter and 3.5 cm (1¹/₂ in) deep. This recipe makes 4–6 cupcakes. Bake for about 20 minutes until cakes are firm to the touch. Cool, then remove cakes from baking cups. Set aside.

Prepare sorbet. Bring water, sugar and glucose to a boil, then lower heat and simmer for 5 minutes. Remove from heat, stir in stabilizer and leave to cool. Combine cooled syrup with passion fruit purée. Mix well and churn using an ice cream machine according to the manufacturer's instructions. Alternatively, mix sorbet in a pre-frozen bowl. Place in the freezer for about 2 hours, then remove and beat to break up newly formed ice crystals. Return to the freezer and allow sorbet to harden slightly. Repeat to break up ice crystals before freezing again. Takes at least 6 hours.

Prepare fruit. Split vanilla bean lengthwise and scrape seeds into a small bowl. Add honey and mix well. Add fruit and toss gently. Cover and refrigerate until needed.

Serve angel food cakes with passion fruit sorbet and vanilla-marinated fruit. Dust with icing sugar and garnish as desired.

## Green Orchard Fruit with Pineapple and Lemon Grass Jelly and Mousse

Preparation Time: 2 hours   Cooking Time: 10 minutes   Serves 4

### FRUIT

**Pear** *1, cored and cut into thick slices*

**Green apple** *1, cored and cut into thick slices*

**Kiwis** *2, peeled and cut into thick chunks*

**Honeydew melon** *450 g (1 lb), rind and seeds removed, cut into thin slices*

**Green grapes** *140 g (5 oz), peeled, seeded and halved*

**Starfruit** *1, sliced*

### JELLY

**Pineapple purée** *180 g (6¹/₂ oz)*

**Fresh lemon grass** *180 g (6¹/₂ oz), bruised and cut into 1-cm (¹/₂-in) rounds*

**Gelatine sheets** *8 leaves, softened in ice water*

**Organic honey** *60 ml (2 fl oz / 4 Tbsp)*

### MOUSSE (OPTIONAL)

**Freshly squeezed pineapple juice** *250 ml (8 fl oz / 1 cup)*

**Lemon grass** *55 g (2 oz), crushed and cut into 1-cm (¹/₂-in) rounds*

**Gelatine sheets** *3 leaves, softened in ice water*

**Organic honey** *5 tsp*

### GARNISH

**Mint leaves** *8*

Prepare jelly. Bring pineapple purée and lemon grass to a boil. Squeeze excess liquid from softened gelatine sheets and add gelatine to pineapple purée. The purée must be hot enough for the gelatine to dissolve. Strain and stir in honey. Remove from heat and leave to cool.

Prepare mousse (optional). Bring pineapple juice and lemon grass to a boil, then pass juice through a fine mesh sieve. Squeeze excess liquid from softened gelatine sheets and add to juice. Leave to cool, then refrigerate for about 30 minutes to thicken mousse before pouring into a siphon. This mousse requires the siphon to produce a dense, creamy texture.

Arrange fruit on individual serving plates and drizzle some half-set jelly over. Serve with mousse (if using) and garnish with mint leaves.

# Citrus-Scented Spa Cheesecake with Orange-Macadamia Nut Brittle

Start preparations 4 hours ahead   Cooking Time: 1 hour 30 minutes   Serves 4

### CHEESECAKES

Ricotta cheese *350 g (12 oz)*

Low-fat cream cheese *350 g (12 oz)*

1-for-1 sweetener *100 g (3¹/₃ oz)*

Half-and-half *250 ml (8 fl oz / 1 cup), or to desired consistency*

Orange *1, finely grated for zest*

Lemon *1, finely grated for zest*

Egg whites *350 g (12 oz)*

### SAUCES

Strawberries *450 g (1 lb), cleaned and hulled*

Orange juice *500 ml (16 fl oz / 2 cups)*

### ORANGE-MACADAMIA NUT BRITTLE

Fine sugar *110 g (4 oz)*

Corn syrup *55 g (2 oz)*

Water *2 Tbsp*

Margarine *2 Tbsp*

Macadamia nuts *110 g (4 oz), coarsely chopped*

Vanilla essence *1 tsp*

Bicarbonate of soda *¹/₂ tsp*

Fine salt *¹/₄ tsp*

Orange *1, finely grated for zest*

**NOTE**

1-for-1 sweetener is a powdered artificial sweetener that has been formulated such that 1 tsp sweetener powder is equivalent to the sweetness of 1 tsp sugar but with fewer calories.

Half-and-half is a dairy product that can be bought off the shelf. It is made up of equal parts of cream and whole milk and is a lighter alternative to cream with a milk fat content of 10–12 per cent.

Prepare cheesecake(s). Line individual moulds, 8.5 cm (3¹/₂ in) in diameter and 3.5 cm (1¹/₂ in) deep, or a 20-cm (8-in) cake pan with parchment paper. Preheat oven to 180°C (350°F).

Beat ricotta, cream cheese and sweetener in a cake mixer until smooth. With the mixer on low, slowly add half-and-half and orange and lemon zest. Add egg whites and continue mixing on low until egg whites are incorporated. Mixing on low speed helps avoid introducing too much air into mixture. Pour mixture into individual moulds or cake pan and place into a large, deep baking tray. Fill tray with water so water comes up one-quarter the sides of moulds or cake pan.

Bake for 30–45 minutes until centre of cake is slightly firm. A skewer inserted into the centre of cake should come out clean. Bake longer if necessary. Set aside to cool.

Prepare sauces. Purée strawberries in a blender (food processor) and strain through a fine mesh sieve. Refrigerate until cold before serving. Bring orange juice to a boil and reduce to 120 ml (4 fl oz / ¹/₂ cup) over low heat. Refrigerate until cold before serving. Takes about 3 hours.

Prepare orange macadamia nut brittle. Combine sugar, corn syrup and water in a pot and bring to a boil over medium heat. Cook until mixture reaches 115°C (240°F) on a candy thermometer or until sugar just starts to develop a light golden colour. Carefully add margarine and stir until dissolved, and then add remaining ingredients, stirring quickly. Remove from heat and pour mixture onto a large sheet of parchment paper. Leave to cool before breaking into pieces.

Remove cooled cheesecake(s) from moulds or cake pan and decorate with brittle. Serve with strawberry and orange sauces.

## Organic Chocolate Cupcakes with Soy Ganache Frosting

Preparation Time: 1 hour 30 minutes   Cooking Time: 40 minutes   Serves 4

### CUPCAKES

Organic plain (all-purpose) flour *70 g (2¹/₂ oz), sifted*

Bicarbonate of soda *³/₄ tsp*

Fine salt *¹/₈ tsp*

Margarine *125 g (4¹/₂ oz)*

Fine sugar *85 g (3 oz)*

Organic cocoa powder *2 Tbsp*

Boiling water *60 ml (2 fl oz / 4 Tbsp)*

Egg *1, lightly beaten*

Vanilla essence *¹/₂ tsp*

Buttermilk *125 ml (4¹/₂ fl oz / ¹/₂ cup)*

### SOY GANACHE FROSTING

Organic soymilk *375 ml (12 fl oz / 1¹/₂ cups)*

68% organic chocolate *180 g (6¹/₂ oz), chopped*

### CHOCOLATE SAUCE

Organic soymilk *250 ml (8 fl oz / 1 cup)*

64% organic chocolate *85 g (3 oz)*

### GARNISH

Raspberries *24*

White chocolate shavings

Prepare cupcakes. Preheat oven to 160°C (325°F). In a medium bowl, combine flour, bicarbonate of soda and salt. Mix well and set aside. Using an electric mixer, whisk margarine and sugar on medium speed to form a grainy paste.

In a small bowl, combine cocoa powder and boiling water. Stir until smooth. Add cocoa mixture, egg and vanilla to margarine and sugar. Blend well to form a smooth batter. Add flour mixture and buttermilk. Blend at low speed until well combined.

Fill 4 non-stick muffin cups 8.5 cm (3¹/₂ in) in diameter and 4 cm (1³/₄ in) deep with batter. Bake for 15–20 minutes, rotating muffin pan halfway through baking. Leave cakes to cool before removing from muffin pan.

Prepare soy ganache frosting. In a small saucepan, bring organic soymilk to a boil. Pour over chocolate and mix with a paddle until chocolate is completely melted. Cool refrigerated for 1 hour, stirring every 15 minutes. Using a paddle, whip mixture quickly for around 10 seconds. Pour frosting into a piping bag fitted with a round tip to decorate cupcakes.

Prepare chocolate sauce. Heat soymilk in a double boiler. Add chocolate and stir until dissolved. Set aside to cool.

Decorate cupcakes with soy ganache frosting and raspberries. Serve with chocolate sauce.

## Caramelised Pineapple Napoleon with Coconut Custard and Vanilla-Tapioca Sauce

Preparation Time: 1 hour   Cooking Time: 2 hours 25 minutes   Serves 4

### PINEAPPLE

Organic honey *220 g (8 oz)*

Vanilla bean *1, split lengthwise*

Water *60 ml (2 fl oz / 4 Tbsp)*

Pineapple flesh *500 g (1 lb 1¹/₂ oz),*
*cut into 1-cm (¹/₂-in) cubes*

### CUSTARD

Skimmed milk *250 ml (8 fl oz / 1 cup)*

Coconut milk *250 ml (8 fl oz / 1 cup)*

Fine sugar *85 g (3 oz)*

Plain (all-purpose) flour *30 g (1 oz)*

Egg yolks *6*

### TAPIOCA SAUCE

Fine sugar *70 g (2¹/₂ oz)*

Instant tapioca *45 g (1¹/₂ oz)*

Skimmed milk *500 ml (16 fl oz / 2 cups)*

Vanilla bean *1, split lengthwise*

### PASTRY LAYERS

Frozen puff pastry *2–3 sheets, left at room*
*temperature for 5 minutes, or use filo pastry*

Icing (confectioners') sugar *45 g (1¹/₂ oz)*

### PINEAPPLE CHIPS

Pineapple flesh *8 thin slices*

Icing (confectioners') sugar *55 g (2 oz)*

**NOTE**
Instant tapioca is processed from tapioca flour. These granules are neutral in taste and can be used in both sweet and savoury preparations such as puddings, pie fillings, soups and gravies.

Prepare pineapple. In a clean and dry medium sauté pan, bring honey, vanilla bean and water to a boil, then cook over medium heat until golden brown. Carefully add pineapple cubes and stir until mixture returns to a boil. Lower heat and simmer for 5 minutes. Remove pineapple and continue to cook liquid over low heat until it reaches the consistency of syrup. Takes about 30 minutes. Strain syrup and set aside to cool.

Prepare custard. Place skimmed milk and coconut milk in a pot and bring to a boil. Whisk sugar, flour and egg yolks in a bowl. Once milk is boiling, add a quarter to egg yolk mixture and whisk until smooth. Add egg yolk mixture to pot of milk and stir over medium heat until it just returns to a boil. Remove from heat and pour into a shallow pan. Cover loosely with plastic wrap (cling film) and refrigerate until cold.

Prepare tapioca sauce. Place all ingredients in a medium pan and bring very slowly to a boil. Lower heat and simmer for 5 minutes, then remove from heat. Discard vanilla bean and leave sauce to cool.

Prepare pastry layers. If using puff pastry, cut 12 rectangles from puff pastry sheets. Vary the size according to preference. Place rectangles on a baking tray lined with parchment paper. Dust with icing sugar and place a sheet of paper and another baking tray on top to prevent puff pastry from rising unevenly when baking. If using filo pastry, brush filo pastry with butter and sandwich 2 layers of filo pastry together before cutting out 20 rectangles. Place rectangles on a baking tray lined with parchment paper. Dust with icing sugar.

Place tray in the centre of a preheated oven and bake at 200°C (400°F) for 20–25 minutes or until pastry is golden brown.

Prepare pineapple chips. Dust pineapple slices with icing sugar on both sides, then place on a greased baking tray or silicon mat. Bake in a 120°C (250°F) oven until chips are light golden in colour. Takes 45 minutes–1 hour. Remove and cool on a wire rack. Chips will crisp upon cooling.

To assemble, pipe custard onto a pastry rectangle. Sandwich with another pastry rectangle. If using puff pastry, continue until 3 layers are achieved. If using filo pastry, continue until 4 layers are achieved. Repeat to make 4 napoleons. Serve with pineapple cubes, tapioca sauce and pineapple syrup. Garnish with pineapple chips.

# Warm Roasted Tropical Fruit with Beet Jus and Lemon-Lime Sorbet

Start preparations 1 day ahead   Cooking Time: 40 minutes   Serves 4

### LEMON-LIME SORBET

Water *450 ml (14¹/₂ fl oz)*

Fine sugar *200 g (7 oz)*

Lime *1, finely grated for zest*

Lemon *1, finely grated for zest*

Lime juice *90 ml (3 fl oz / 6 Tbsp)*

Lemon juice *90 ml (3 fl oz / 6 Tbsp)*

### BEET JUS

Beetroot *180 g (6¹/₂ oz), peeled and roughly sliced*

Water *210 ml (7 fl oz)*

Fine sugar *55 g (2 oz)*

Corn flour (cornstarch) *2 Tbsp, mixed with 75 ml (2¹/₂ fl oz / 5 Tbsp) water*

### ROASTED FRUIT

Olive oil *3 Tbsp*

Mango flesh *45 g (1¹/₂ oz), cut into 4 equal pieces*

Banana *30 g (1 oz), peeled and cut in 4 equal pieces*

Jackfruit *30 g (1 oz), cut into 4 equal pieces*

Longan *30 g (1 oz), weighed without seeds*

Vanilla bean *¹/₂*

Ground black pepper *¹/₂ tsp*

Fine sugar *1 tsp*

Organic honey *¹/₂ Tbsp*

Red chilli *1, split lengthwise in half*

Lemon grass (see Glossary) *15 g (¹/₂ oz), ends trimmed, hard outer leaves removed, use only bulbous end, pounded*

### TUILE

Margarine *30 g (1 oz), melted*

Icing (confectioners') sugar *30 g (1 oz)*

Plain (all-purpose) flour *30 g (1 oz)*

Egg white *30 g (1 oz)*

Prepare lemon-lime sorbet. Bring water and sugar to a boil and simmer for 5 minutes. Remove from heat and leave to cool. When cool, stir in lime and lemon zests and juices. Mix well and churn in an ice cream maker according to the manufacturer's instructions.

Prepare beet jus. Cook beetroot in water over low heat for 20 minutes, then place mixture in a blender (food processor) and purée until smooth. Strain jus and reheat over medium heat. Stir in sugar until dissolved. Add corn flour mixture and stir to achieve the consistency of a thick sauce.

Prepare roasted fruit. Heat olive oil in a large pan. Sauté fruit with vanilla bean, pepper, sugar, honey, chilli and lemon grass over high heat until lightly browned. The fruit should still retain their shape and be firm on the inside. Remove lemon grass and vanilla bean. Keep fruit warm.

Prepare tuile dough. Using a cake mixer, combine all ingredients on low speed until a smooth batter is achieved. Spread batter in a thin layer on a greased baking tray or silicon mat. Bake in a preheated oven at 200°C (400°F) until golden brown. Takes 2–4 minutes. While still hot, cut a thin rectangular slice, measuring 10 cm x 2 cm (4 in x 1 in), and wrap it around a large round mould. Once cold, tuile will harden. Slide carefully from mould and store in an airtight container. Repeat to make more tuiles.

Drizzle beet jus over fruit and serve with lemon-lime sorbet and tuile.

## Chilled Lemon Myrtle and Mint Soup with Frozen Green Tea Yoghurt

Start preparations 1½ days ahead   Cooking Time: 8 minutes
Freezing time: 6 hours or until firm by hand; 30–40 minutes if using an ice cream machine   Serves 4

### HONEY SYRUP

Water *180 ml (6 fl oz)*

Organic honey *150 g (5⅓ oz)*

Lime juice *1 tsp*

### SOUP

Cantaloupe flesh *450 g (1 lb), puréed*

Lemon myrtle oil *10 drops*

Chopped mint leaves *1 Tbsp*

Lemon juice *90 ml (3 fl oz / 6 Tbsp)*

Orange juice *90 ml (3 fl oz / 6 Tbsp)*

### FROZEN GREEN TEA YOGHURT

Buttermilk *60 ml (2 fl oz / 4 Tbsp)*

Greek yoghurt *250 g (9 oz)*

Japanese green tea powder *1 Tbsp*

Organic honey *55 g (2 oz)*

**NOTE**
Lemon myrtle oil is an essential oil extracted from the steam distillation of fresh lemon myrtle leaves. It has a unique citrus flavour and aroma similar to a blend of lemon grass, lime and lemon.

Prepare honey syrup. Bring water and honey to a boil, then lower heat and simmer for 5 minutes. Stir in lime juice and remove from heat. Leave to cool.

Prepare soup. Combine ingredients for soup and stir in honey syrup. Refrigerate overnight.

Prepare frozen green tea yoghurt. Combine all ingredients for frozen yoghurt and mix well until green tea powder is dissolved. Churn in an ice cream maker according to the manufacturer's instructions. Alternatively, mix frozen yoghurt in a pre-frozen bowl. Place in the freezer for about 2 hours, then remove and beat to break up newly formed ice crystals. Return to the freezer and allow frozen yoghurt to harden slightly. Repeat to break up ice crystals before freezing again. Takes at least 6 hours.

Serve frozen green tea yoghurt with chilled soup. Garnish as desired.

## Lemon Pudding Cakes with Berry Consommé and Vanilla Sherbet

Start preparations 1½ days ahead   Cooking Time: 1 hour 40 minutes

Sherbet Freezing Time: 6 hours or until firm by hand; 30–40 minutes using an ice cream machine   Serves 4

### BERRY CONSOMMÉ

**Strawberries** *500 g (1 lb 1½ oz), hulled and quartered*

**Raspberries** *250 g (9 oz)*

**Blackberries** *250 g (9 oz)*

**Organic honey** *100 g (3½ oz)*

**Vanilla bean** *1, split lengthwise*

### VANILLA SHERBET

**Vanilla bean** *1, split lengthwise and seeds scraped*

**Water** *300 ml (10 fl oz / 1¼ cups)*

**Fine sugar** *220 g (8 oz)*

**Skimmed milk** *300 ml (10 fl oz / 1¼ cups)*

### LEMON PUDDING CAKES

**Margarine** *70 g (2½ oz)*

**1-for-1 sweetener (see Note on pg 148)** *85 g (3 oz)*

**Eggs** *5, whites and yolks separated*

**Plain (all-purpose) flour** *45 g (1½ oz)*

**Skimmed milk** *250 ml (8 fl oz / 1 cup)*

**Lemon juice** *180 ml (6 fl oz / ¾ cup)*

**Lemon** *1, finely grated for zest*

**Fine sugar** *85 g (3 oz)*

### GARNISH

**Strawberries** *8*

**Raspberries** *16*

**Blackberries** *16*

**Mint leaves** *16*

Prepare berry consommé. Place all ingredients in a heatproof (flameproof) bowl, cover with plastic wrap (cling film) and place over a pot of hot water on a rack. Double-boil over medium heat for 40 minutes or until all the juice is extracted from the berries and berries are light in colour. Drain juice into a bowl and refrigerate until ready to use.

Prepare vanilla sherbet. Combine vanilla seeds, water, sugar and milk in a saucepan and bring to a boil. Remove from heat and leave to rest for 15 minutes. Strain and cool, then churn using an ice cream maker according to the manufacturer's directions. Alternatively, mix sherbet in a pre-frozen bowl. Place in the freezer for about 2 hours, then remove and beat to break up newly formed ice crystals. Return to the freezer and allow sherbet to harden slightly. Repeat to break up ice crystals before freezing again. Takes at least 6 hours.

Prepare lemon pudding cakes. Preheat oven to 170°C (330°F). Grease and dust four 110 g (4 oz) baking cups with sugar. Using an electric cake mixer, beat margarine and sweetener until fluffy. Takes about 5 minutes. Add egg yolks one at a time, scraping the bowl each time. Beat in flour, milk, lemon juice and zest, until well combined. Set aside.

In another mixing bowl, beat egg whites until frothy. Slowly add sugar and beat until stiff peaks form. Fold in egg yolk mixture just until combined.

Fill prepared moulds to the brim with batter. Place moulds in a deep baking tray and fill with water until water comes one-quarter up the sides of moulds. Place in the oven to bake until puddings are set. Takes about 35 minutes. Leave puddings to cool, then refrigerate overnight.

Serve lemon pudding cakes with berry consommé and vanilla sherbet. Garnish as desired.

# Smoothies

Nourishing combinations of impeccably fresh fruit and vegetables which are blended into thick, wholesome drinks, *Naturally Peninsula* smoothies are delicious and refreshing — a great source of health on the go with its high vitamin, mineral and fibre content. For a morning jump-start, a midday energy boost or an after-dinner treat, these smoothies are an easy and satisfying way to ingest a valuable serving of healthy ingredients. Just take in all the natural goodness of a *Naturally Peninsula* smoothie in a few gulps and you will be ready to conquer the world!

## Pumpkin Smoothie

Preparation Time: 10 minutes   Cooking Time: Nil   Makes about 300 ml (10 fl oz / 1¼ cups)

**Pumpkin flesh** *110 g (4 oz)*

**Bananas** *110 g (4 oz), peeled*

**Orange juice** *180 ml (6 fl oz / ¾ cup)*

**Ground cinnamon** *¼ tsp*

Combine all ingredients in a blender (food processor) and blend until smooth. Pour into a chilled glass and serve immediately.

## Cucumber Mint Smoothie

Preparation Time: 10 minutes   Cooking Time: Nil   Makes about 300 ml (10 fl oz / 1¼ cups)

**Apples** *140 g (5 oz), peeled, cored and cut*

**Mint leaves** *6 sprigs*

**Lemon sherbet** *85 g (3 oz)*

**Cucumber** *200 g (7 oz) peeled and seeded*

Pass apples through a juicer to obtain about 90 ml (3 fl oz / 6 Tbsp) juice. Pour juice into a blender (food processor) with mint leaves, lemon sherbet and cucumber and blend until smooth. Pour into a chilled glass and serve immediately.

## Antioxidant Smoothie

Preparation Time: 10 minutes   Cooking Time: Nil   Makes about 270 ml (9 fl oz)

**Strawberries** *55 g (2 oz)*

**Blueberries** *45 g (1½ oz)*

**Raspberries** *55 g (2 oz)*

**Skimmed milk** *125 ml (4 fl oz / ½ cup)*

Combine all ingredients in a blender (food processor) and blend for 30 seconds until smooth. Pour into a chilled glass and serve immediately.

*From left to right: Pumpkin Smoothie, Cucumber Mint Smoothie, Antioxidant Smoothie*

## All-in-One Smoothie

Preparation Time: 10 minutes   Cooking Time: Nil   Makes about 260 ml (9 fl oz)

Bananas *110 g (4 oz), peeled*
Greek yoghurt *55 g (2 oz)*
Skimmed milk *125 ml (4 fl oz / 1/2 cup)*
Organic honey *10 g (1/3 oz)*
Flaxseed *10 g (1/2 oz)*

Combine all ingredients in a blender (food processor) and blend until smooth.
Pour into a chilled glass and serve immediately.

## Papaya Banana Smoothie

Preparation Time: 15 minutes   Cooking Time: Nil   Makes about 300 ml (10 fl oz / 1 1/4 cups)

Papaya *140 g (5 oz), peeled and seeded*
Plain yoghurt *2 Tbsp*
Orange juice *125 ml (4 fl oz / 1/2 cup)*
Bananas *100 g (3 1/2 oz), peeled*
Organic honey *1 Tbsp*

Combine all ingredients in a blender (food processor) and blend until smooth.
Pour into a chilled glass and serve immediately.

## Cantaloupe Smoothie

Preparation Time: 10 minutes   Cooking Time: Nil   Makes about 300 ml (10 fl oz / 1 1/4 cups)

Cantaloupe flesh *110 g (4 oz), peeled and seeded*
Bananas *85 g (3 oz), peeled*
Skimmed milk *90 ml (3 fl oz / 6 Tbsp)*
Organic honey *1 Tbsp*
Plain yoghurt *2 Tbsp*

Combine all ingredients in a blender (food processor) and blend until smooth.
Pour into a chilled glass and serve immediately.

*Clockwise from top: All-in-One Smoothie, Papaya Banana Smoothie, Cantaloupe Smoothie*

## Vitamin Booster Smoothie

Preparation Time: 10 minutes   Cooking Time: Nil   Makes about 270 ml (9 fl oz)

Pineapple flesh *70 g (2¹/₂ oz)*

Oranges *120 g (4¹/₂ oz), peeled*

Ginger *6 g (¹/₅ oz), peeled*

Canned lychees *85 g (3 oz)*

Olive oil *2 tsp*

Combine ingredients in a blender (food processor) and blend for about 1 minute until smooth. Serve immediately at room temperature or poured over crushed ice.


## Cholesterol Fighter Smoothie

Preparation Time: 10 minutes   Cooking Time: Nil   Makes about 270 ml (9 fl oz)

Carrots *140 g (5 oz), peeled and cut into shorter lengths*

Celery *100 g (3¹/₂ oz), cut into shorter lengths*

Apples *140 g (5 oz), cut into quarters*

Greek non-fat plain yoghurt *70 g (2¹/₂ oz)*

Pass carrots, celery and apples through a juicer to obtain about 180 ml (6 fl oz / ³/₄ cup) juice in total.

Add yoghurt to mixed juice and use a hand blender to fully incorporate yoghurt. Pour into a chilled glass and serve immediately.

*From left: Vitamin Booster Smoothie, Cholesterol Fighter Smoothie*

# Basic Stocks

The base of good cooking is a superior home-made stock and our five basic stock recipes provide the perfect and complete arsenal for the creation of many culinary masterpieces. Do keep the stock pots simmering on the stove for that important *Naturally Peninsula* ingredient!

## Vegetable Stock

Makes about 3 litres (96 fl oz / 12 cups)

**White onions** *300 g (11 oz), peeled and cut into 2.5-cm (1-in) cubes*

**Carrots** *300 g (11 oz), peeled and cut into 2.5-cm (1-in) cubes*

**Leeks** *300 g (11 oz), peeled and cut into 2.5-cm (1-in) cubes*

**Celery** *300 g (11 oz), cut into 2.5-cm (1-in) cubes*

**Cabbage** *300 g (11 oz)*

**Lettuce** *300 g (11 oz)*

**Lemon grass** *55 g (2 oz)*

**Ginger** *55 g (2 oz), peeled*

**Chervil** *55 g (2 oz)*

**Water** *4 litres (128 fl oz / 16 cups)*

**Fine salt** *20 g (²/₃ oz)*

Place all ingredients into a large stockpot and bring slowly to a boil. Lower heat and simmer for about 1 hour.

Strain through a cloth-lined strainer. Leave to cool. Store refrigerated.

## Lamb Jus

Makes about 1 litre (32 fl oz / 4 cups)

**Carrot** *55 g (2 oz), peeled and cut into 2.5-cm (1-in) cubes*

**Onion** *45 g (1¹/₂ oz), peeled and cut into 2.5-cm (1-in) cubes*

**Celery** *45 g (1¹/₂ oz), cut into 2.5-cm (1-in) cubes*

**Corn oil** *2 Tbsp*

**Garlic** *3 cloves, peeled and left whole*

**Tomato paste** *55 g (2 oz)*

**Canned peeled tomatoes** *85 g (3 oz)*

**Red wine** *210 ml (7 fl oz)*

**Rosemary** *4 sprigs*

**Thyme** *4 sprigs*

**Bay leaves** *2*

**Lamb bones** *1 kg (2 lb 3 oz)*

**Water** *2 litres (64 fl oz / 8 cups)*

**Port wine** *105 ml (3¹/₂ fl oz)*

**Cold butter** *30 g (1 oz)*

**Fine salt** *¹/₄ tsp*

**Ground black pepper** *¹/₈ tsp*

In a stockpot, sauté carrot, onion, celery and garlic in corn oil until onion is translucent. Add tomato paste and canned peeled tomatoes. After 1 minute, deglaze (see Note on pg 54) with red wine and add rosemary, thyme and bay leaves.

Add bones and water and bring to a boil, then lower heat and simmer for about 2 hours. Skim off any froth that surfaces during the process.

Strain stock through a cloth-lined strainer, then reduce with port wine over low heat to about 1 litre (32 fl oz / 4 cups). Stir in cold butter, then season with salt and pepper.

## Chicken Stock

Makes about 1 litre (32 fl oz / 4 cups)

Water *4 litres (128 fl oz / 16 cups)*

Chicken bones *2 kg (4 lb 6 oz), chopped and rinsed; soaked for 30 minutes*

Leek *100 g (3 1/2 oz), use white part, peeled and cut into 2.5-cm (1-in) cubes*

Carrot *55 g (2 oz), peeled and cut into 2.5-cm (1-in) cubes*

Onion *55 g (2 oz), peeled and cut into 2.5-cm (1-in) cubes*

Celery *55 g (2 oz), cut into 2.5-cm (1-in) cubes*

Parsley *10 sprigs*

Thyme *5 stalks*

White peppercorns *1 Tbsp*

Bring water to a boil and blanch chicken bones for 2 minutes over high heat.

Lower heat and skim off any scum from surface of stock. Add remaining ingredients and simmer over low heat for 1 hour.

Strain through a fine mesh sieve and return to the pot. Reduce to 1 litre (32 fl oz / 4 cups) over low heat. Leave to cool. Store refrigerated.

## Fish Stock

Makes about 1 litre (32 fl oz / 4 cups)

Fish bones *500 g (1 lb 1 1/2 oz), cleaned, chopped in small pieces and rinsed*

Onion *85 g (3 oz), peeled and sliced*

Celery *85 g (3 oz), sliced*

Leek *85 g (3 oz), sliced*

White peppercorns *1 Tbsp, crushed*

Bay leaf *1*

White wine *105 ml ( 3 1/2 fl oz)*

Cold water *1.2 litres (40 fl oz / 5 cups)*

Place all ingredients into a stockpot and bring to a boil. When water comes to a boil, lower heat and simmer for 20 minutes. Skim off any scum from surface of stock.

Strain through a fine mesh sieve and return to the pot. Reduce to 1 litre (32 fl oz / 4 cups) over low heat. Leave to cool. Store refrigerated.

## Veal Stock

Makes about 1 litre (32 fl oz / 4 cups)

Water *4 litres (128 fl oz / 16 cups)*

Veal bones *2 kg (4 lb 6 oz), chopped and rinsed for 30 minutes*

Leek *105 g (3½ oz), use white part, cut into 2.5-cm (1-in) cubes*

Carrot *55 g (2 oz), peeled and cut into 2.5-cm (1-in) cubes*

Onion *55 g (2 oz), peeled and cut into 2.5-cm (1-in) cubes*

Celery *55 g (2 oz), cut into 2.5-cm (1-in) cubes*

Parsley *10 sprigs*

Thyme *5 sprigs*

White peppercorns *1 Tbsp*

Bring water to a boil and blanch veal bones in water for 4 minutes over high heat.

Lower heat and skim off any scum from surface of stock. Add remaining ingredients and simmer over low heat for 1 hour.

Strain through a fine mesh sieve and return to the pot. Reduce to 1 litre (32 fl oz / 4 cups) over low heat. Leave to cool. Store refrigerated.

# Kitchen Techniques

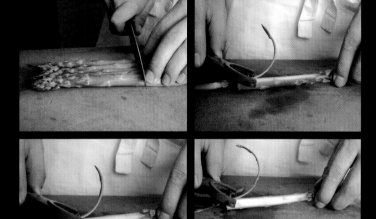

How to clean mature asparagus: Mature asparagus spears have a fibrous outer layer that can be unpleasant to bite into. To clean them, first cut off about 5 cm (2 in) from the lower end of each spear, then use a Y-shaped vegetable peeler to remove all of the outer layer, starting from just under the tip.

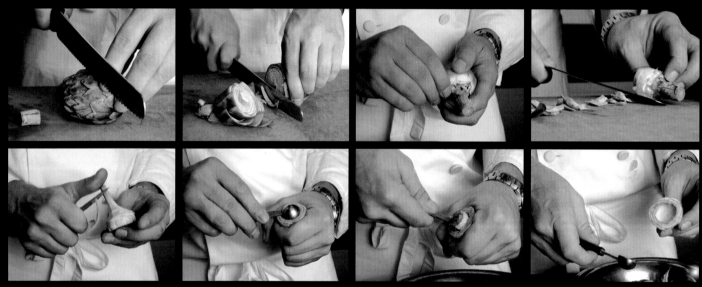

How to clean artichokes: Trim the stem of the artichoke, leaving about 2.5 cm (1 in) behind. Use a serrated knife to cut off the top half of the artichoke, then remove the darker, outer leaves from the lower half by bending them backwards until they snap off. Use a sharp paring knife to remove the lighter, inner leaves by cutting them off at the base, then peel off the fibrous outer layer of the stem. Use a melon baller to scoop out the fuzzy centre to discard, then soak cleaned artichoke in a bowl of ice water mixed with the juice of a lemon and 1 tsp salt to prevent discolouration. Alternatively, replace salt with some flat-leaf (Italian) parsley.

How to make tri-coloured pasta for vegetable lasagne: Prepare 3 types — plain (yellow), beetroot (purple) and parsley (green) — of pasta dough (see pg 133). With each type of dough, flatten it on a floured work surface with floured hands, then pass it through a pasta machine several times until the result is 0.2-cm (1/10-in) thick. Cut rolled out plain dough into 5-cm (2-in) squares, then transfer them to a floured tray, cover with plastic wrap (cling film) and set aside. Cut rolled out beetroot and parsley doughs into 1-cm (1/2-in) wide strips. Onto each plain dough square, lay two green strips, one at each end, and one purple strip across the centre. Secure strips with a little egg wash and trim off uneven edges.

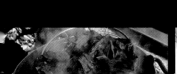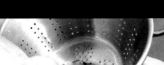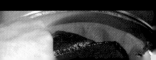

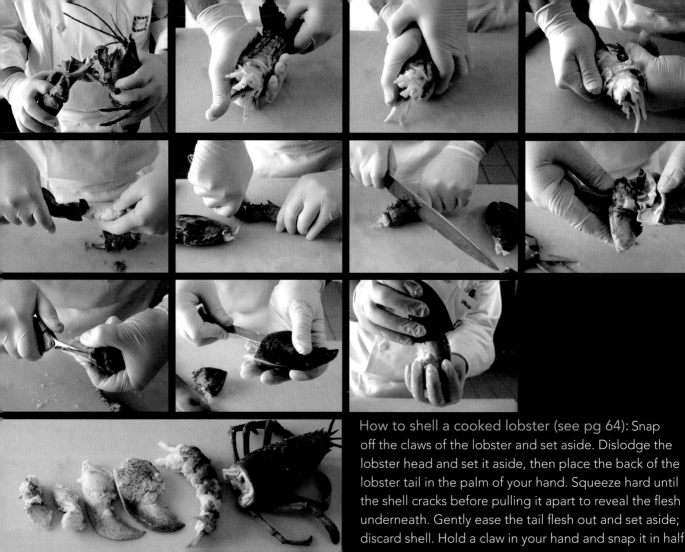

How to shell a cooked lobster (see pg 64): Snap off the claws of the lobster and set aside. Dislodge the lobster head and set it aside, then place the back of the lobster tail in the palm of your hand. Squeeze hard until the shell cracks before pulling it apart to reveal the flesh underneath. Gently ease the tail flesh out and set aside; discard shell. Hold a claw in your hand and snap it in half

How to make garlic cream cappuccino (see pg 141): Sauté shallots, garlic, thyme and bay leaf in butter until shallots are translucent, but not browned. Add white wine and bring to a boil before adding chicken stock and cream. Stir through and reduce liquid by half over medium-low heat. Remove and discard thyme and bay leaf, then pour remaining liquid and solid ingredients into a blender (food processor) to purée. Strain puréed mixture by passing through a fine mesh sieve into a clean saucepan, then season lightly with salt and pepper. Use a hand-held blender to blend in remaining butter, a little at a time, until butter is fully incorporated and sauce is foamy.

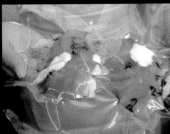

Poaching chicken in a vacuum bag (see pg 24): Season chicken with salt and pepper. Place into a vacuum bag with thyme and some peeled, sliced garlic for extra flavour, if desired. Place filled bag in the vacuum-packing machine and wait until all the air is sucked out and the bag is sealed. Heat a large pot of water to 70°C (155°F), then lower bag into water and allow to simmer for about 20 minutes or until chicken is just cooked. Maintain the temperature of the water at 70°C (155°F) throughout the cooking process. This technique can be applied to veal as well (see pg 108). If you do not have a vacuum-packing machine, sandwich bags will do as well.

Lemon Grass

Frisée

Fennel

Flat-leaf (Italian) Parsley

Celeriac

Hot Basil Leaves

Kaffir Lime Leaves

Kohlrabi

Couscous

Quinoa

Broad (Fava) Beans

# Glossary

## GREENS AND HERBS

**Celeriac Root** Also known as celery root, this versatile vegetable is the root of a special celery cultivated specifically for its root, and can be eaten raw or cooked. It ranges in size from a common apple to a small melon and has white flesh which tastes similar to a blend of celery and parsley. Choose firm and small to medium-size celeriac.

**Fennel** This vegetable consists of a broad bulbous base with short stalks and feathery leaves. Recipes calling for fennel usually use the bulb, which has a light and sweet aromatic flavour reminiscent of anise. Fennel can be eaten raw or cooked. Choose smaller bulbs as this means they are younger and less fibrous.

**Frisée** The spiky shape of its leaves makes frisée easily distinguishable from other salad greens. It holds its shape well and does not wilt easily. This firmness of texture and its mild bitter taste add contrast to salads, making frisée a popular salad green.

**Flat-leaf (Italian) Parsley** This herb is appreciated for its fresh, slightly peppery flavour and is used both as a garnish and flavouring. It has a richer flavour and more pungent aroma than its curly-leaf counterpart. Choose parsley with full bright green leaves and stems that have a fresh scent. Moisture causes the leaves to rot easily, so dry well before refrigerating.

**Hot Basil Leaves** Also known as holy basil, this variety of basil is distinguished by its jagged leaves which have a peppery taste with a hint of mint and cloves. It is widely used in Thai cooking.

**Kaffir Lime Leaves** These dark green leaves are stiff and glossy and a single leaf looks like two leaves joined end to end. Its fresh citrus aroma withstands freezing, making the frozen leaves a good substitute for the fresh. Dried leaves are much less flavourful, so use twice as many as the recipe calls for when substituting them for fresh leaves.

**Kohlrabi** This vegetable is a member of the turnip family. The bulb has light green skin and crunchy flesh with a naturally sweet and delicate flavour similar to that of mild, sweet turnip. Choose small bulbs as they tend to be sweeter and more tender.

**Lemon Grass** This is a tall grass with a bulbous base and is widely used in Thai and Vietnamese cooking. When using, remove the hard outer leaves, trim the ends and use only the bulbous lower portion. Lemon grass has a refreshing and distinctive citrus flavour. The bulb should be bruised or pounded before cooking to fully release its flavour and aroma.

## GRAINS AND PULSES

**Broad (Fava) Beans** When choosing fresh broad beans in pods, select those where the beans are not bulging from the pods, as this indicates younger, more tender beans. The beans have very tough skin which can be removed by blanching briefly in boiling water.

**Couscous** This pasta is made from coarsely ground durum wheat (semolina). It can be steamed or boiled like rice. Instant couscous takes just 10 minutes to cook while the traditional variety takes at least 2 hours. Couscous is a staple food in the Middle East and North Africa, where it is commonly served with meat or vegetable stews.

**Quinoa** A tiny, ivory-coloured grain that is rich in protein. It is easy to prepare and takes on a light, fluffy texture when cooked. Its mild, slightly nutty flavour makes it an excellent alternative to rice or couscous. When cooked, it swells to four times its original size.

Chinese Wolfberries

Pomegranates

Thai Bird's Eye Chillies

Thai Rosella

Ancho Chillies

Kalamansi Limes

Straw Mushrooms

Chanterelles

Porcini (Cep)

Black Trumpet Mushrooms

Black Périgord Truffles

Morels

Black Fungus, dried

# FRUIT AND FRUIT VEGETABLES

*Ancho Chillies* These are dried poblano chillies. They are broad and short and have a mild hot, sweet flavour. Rehydrate before use by soaking in water for 10–15 minutes. Ancho chillies may be stored in clean, dry airtight containers in the freezer for up to a year.

*Chinese Wolfberries* Chinese wolfberries play an important role in traditional Chinese medicine (TCM). These red berries are believed to enhance the functions of the immune system, improve vision and protect the liver. Chinese wolfberries are sweet, somewhat similar to raisins, and can be used in Chinese soups, brewed in tea or eaten raw.

*Kalamansi Limes* Also spelt "calamansi", these small, round limes have an inviting tangerine fragrance and a very thin green skin that turns orange when ripe. However, kalamansi limes are most commonly used when still green and firm.

*Pomegranates* Pomegranates have a leathery, deep red to purplish red rind. When split apart, a labyrinth of red seeds buried in a mass of inedible spongy white flesh is revealed. Only the seeds, with their sweet-tart flavour, are edible.

*Thai Bird's Eye Chillies* These chillies may be small and slender, but they have been rated the hottest chilli after the habanero. Thai bird's eye chillies are green when unripe and turn red when ripe. Both are enjoyed for their fiery flavour.

*Thai Rosella* This Thai medicinal herb is the calyx of a species of hibiscus. When made into a sauce, the taste and appearance is similar to that of cranberry sauce. Thai rosella can also used in tarts and jams and as a red food colouring.

# MUSHROOMS

*Black Fungus, dried* Also known as wood ear fungus, this is a popular ingredient in Chinese cuisine. Even after cooking, black fungus remains bland, but is enjoyed for its crunchy texture. Soak in water to rehydrate before using.

*Black Périgord Truffles* Named after the Périgord region in France renowned for their black truffles, these dark, round, pungent fungi are amongst the most luxurious and expensive of culinary ingredients. Because of its high price and pungency, black truffles are usually sliced paper-thin and used sparingly.

*Black Trumpet Mushrooms* These distinct trumpet-shaped mushrooms have thin and brittle flesh. They are highly aromatic with a buttery flavour.

*Chanterelles* Chanterelles refer to a whole family of mushrooms, but the most common are the golden or yellow chantarelles, which are enjoyed for their exquisite taste and flavour. Use fresh chanterelles where possible, although dried and canned varieties are available.

*Morels* These wild mushrooms have a unique cone shape with a honeycomb pattern and are available fresh or dried. Morels are enjoyed for their unique nutty, earthy flavour that is more intense in the dried variety.

*Porcini (Cep)* A wild mushroom with a smooth cap and thick stem, the young and smaller porcini are valued more than the mature and large ones as the latter ones are slimy and less tasty. Porcini is enjoyed raw or lightly sautéed. Dried porcini is also often ground and used as a flavouring for stews and gravies.

*Portobello* This is a mushroom that is easily distinguishable by its large, thick cap and stem. It has a musky, earthy flavour and meaty texture that makes it ideal as a meat substitute and stuffing ingredient.

*Straw Mushrooms* These mushrooms look as if they are wearing a long cap that almost covers their stems. This is, however, only because they are usually harvested before the caps have fully opened. Straw mushrooms are commonly available dried or canned. Soak to soften and clean dried mushrooms well before using. If storing excess canned mushrooms after opening, remove from can and store refrigerated in fresh water for a few days.

# Weights and Measures

Quantities for this book are given in Metric and American (spoon and cup) measures. Standard spoon and cup measurements used are: 1 teaspoon = 5 ml, 1 tablespoon = 15 ml, 1 cup = 250 ml. All measures are level unless otherwise stated.

## LIQUID AND VOLUME MEASURES

| Metric | Imperial | American |
|---|---|---|
| 5 ml | $\frac{1}{6}$ fl oz | 1 teaspoon |
| 10 ml | $\frac{1}{3}$ fl oz | 1 dessertspoon |
| 15 ml | $\frac{1}{2}$ fl oz | 1 tablespoon |
| 60 ml | 2 fl oz | $\frac{1}{4}$ cup (4 tablespoons) |
| 85 ml | $2\frac{1}{2}$ fl oz | $\frac{1}{3}$ cup |
| 90 ml | 3 fl oz | $\frac{3}{8}$ cup (6 tablespoons) |
| 125 ml | 4 fl oz | $\frac{1}{2}$ cup |
| 180 ml | 6 fl oz | $\frac{3}{4}$ cup |
| 250 ml | 8 fl oz | 1 cup |
| 300 ml | 10 fl oz ($\frac{1}{2}$ pint) | $1\frac{1}{4}$ cups |
| 375 ml | 12 fl oz | $1\frac{1}{2}$ cups |
| 435 ml | 14 fl oz | $1\frac{3}{4}$ cups |
| 500 ml | 16 fl oz | 2 cups |
| 625 ml | 20 fl oz (1 pint) | $2\frac{1}{2}$ cups |
| 750 ml | 24 fl oz ($1\frac{1}{5}$ pints) | 3 cups |
| 1 litre | 32 fl oz ($1\frac{3}{5}$ pints) | 4 cups |
| 1.25 litres | 40 fl oz (2 pints) | 5 cups |
| 1.5 litres | 48 fl oz ($2\frac{2}{5}$ pints) | 6 cups |
| 2.5 litres | 80 fl oz (4 pints) | 10 cups |

## DRY MEASURES

| Metric | Imperial |
|---|---|
| 30 grams | 1 ounce |
| 45 grams | $1\frac{1}{2}$ ounces |
| 55 grams | 2 ounces |
| 70 grams | $2\frac{1}{2}$ ounces |
| 85 grams | 3 ounces |
| 100 grams | $3\frac{1}{2}$ ounces |
| 110 grams | 4 ounces |
| 125 grams | $4\frac{1}{2}$ ounces |
| 140 grams | 5 ounces |
| 280 grams | 10 ounces |
| 450 grams | 16 ounces (1 pound) |
| 500 grams | 1 pound, $1\frac{1}{2}$ ounces |
| 700 grams | $1\frac{1}{2}$ pounds |
| 800 grams | $1\frac{3}{4}$ pounds |
| 1 kilogram | 2 pounds, 3 ounces |
| 1.5 kilograms | 3 pounds, $4\frac{1}{2}$ ounces |
| 2 kilograms | 4 pounds, 6 ounces |

## OVEN TEMPERATURE

| | °C | °F | Gas Regulo |
|---|---|---|---|
| Very slow | 120 | 250 | 1 |
| Slow | 150 | 300 | 2 |
| Moderately slow | 160 | 325 | 3 |
| Moderate | 180 | 350 | 4 |
| Moderately hot | 190/200 | 370/400 | 5/6 |
| Hot | 210/220 | 410/440 | 6/7 |
| Very hot | 230 | 450 | 8 |
| Super hot | 250/290 | 475/550 | 9/10 |

## LENGTH

| Metric | Imperial |
|---|---|
| 0.5 cm | $\frac{1}{4}$ inch |
| 1 cm | $\frac{1}{2}$ inch |
| 1.5 cm | $\frac{3}{4}$ inch |
| 2.5 cm | 1 inch |

## ABBREVIATION

| | |
|---|---|
| tsp | teaspoon |
| tbsp | tablespoon |
| g | gram |
| kg | kilogram |
| ml | millilitre |

# THE PENINSULA
## HOTELS

*The Peninsula Hong Kong*

*The Peninsula New York*

*The Peninsula Chicago*

*The Peninsula Beverly Hills*

*The Peninsula Bangkok*

*The Peninsula Beijing*

*The Peninsula Manila*

*The Peninsula Tokyo (2007)*

**The Peninsula Hong Kong**
Salisbury Road, Kowloon, Hong Kong
Telephone: (852) 2920 2888 Facsimile: (852) 2722 4170
E-mail: phk@peninsula.com

**The Peninsula New York**
700 Fifth Avenue at 55th Street,
New York, NY 10019, U.S.A.
Telephone: (1-212) 956 2888 Facsimile: (1-212) 903 3949
E-mail: pny@peninsula.com

**The Peninsula Chicago**
108 East Superior Street (at North Michigan Avenue),
Chicago, IL 60611, U.S.A.
Telephone: (1-312) 337 2888 Facsimile: (1-312) 751 2888
E-mail: pch@peninsula.com

**The Peninsula Beverly Hills**
9882 South Santa Monica Boulevard,
Beverly Hills, CA 90212, U.S.A.
Telephone: (1-310) 551 2888 Facsimile: (1-310) 788 2319
E-mail: pbh@peninsula.com

**The Peninsula Bangkok**
333 Charoennakorn Road, Klongsan,
Bangkok 10600, Thailand
Telephone: (66-2) 861 2888 Facsimile: (66-2) 861 1112
E-mail: pbk@peninsula.com

**The Peninsula Beijing**
8 Goldfish Lane, Wangfujing, Beijing 100006,
People's Republic of China
Telephone: (86-10) 8516 2888 Facsimile: (86-10) 6510 6311
E-mail: pbj@peninsula.com

**The Peninsula Manila**
Corner of Ayala & Makati Avenues,
1226 Makati City, Metro Manila, Philippines
Telephone: (63-2) 887 2888 Facsimile: (63-2) 815 4825
E-mail: pmn@peninsula.com

**The Peninsula Tokyo (2007)**
1-8-1 Yurakucho, Chiyoda-ku, Tokyo, 100-0006, Japan
Telephone: (81-3) 6270 2888 Facsimile: (81-3) 6270 2000
E-mail: ptk@peninsula.com

For more information, please visit us at peninsula.com

**Project Coordination**
Paul Tchen and Joanna Ng

**Culinary Coordination**
Florian Trento and Philip Sedgwick

**Project and Recipe Contributors**
Matthias Al-Amiry, Carlo Batucan, Bernd Beitmann, Sumalee Boon-ek, Graham Elliot Bowles, Patrice Cabannes, Chan Wai, Andy Cheng, Anthony Coriell, Michael Corvino, Terry Crandall, Gerhard Doll, Oliver Dudler, Uwe Faust, Miguel Franco, Raymond Garcia, David Goodridge, Sean Hardy, Jennifer Kane, Kwan Keung, Lai Wing Koon, Moky Lam, Taylor Ly, Alex Martinez, Gordon Maybury, Adam Mathis, Michelle Medina, Anuwat Morakotjantachote, Bernhard Muller, Jennings Pang, Joseph Sampermans, Max Santiago, Philip Sedgwick, Lito Song, Amy Sutton, Tam Kwok Fung, Adam Tanner, Dee Ann Tsurumaki, Florian Trento, Maximilian von Reden, Wan Kwok Chung, Oliver Weber and Nathaniel Wride

**Photoshoot Location**
The Peninsula Hong Kong

**The Hongkong and Shanghai Hotels, Limited**
8th Floor, St. George's Building, 2 Ice House Street, Central, Hong Kong
www.hshgroup.com

The Hon Sir Michael Kadoorie, Chairman
Ian D Boyce, Vice Chairman
Clement K M Kwok, Managing Director and Chief Executive Officer
Mark Broadley, Finance Director and Chief Financial Officer
Peter C Borer, Director and Chief Operating Officer

**Peninsula Merchandising Limited**
8th Floor, St. George's Building, 2 Ice House Street, Central, Hong Kong
www.peninsulaboutique.com

Paul Tchen, General Manager
Martin Yim, Merchandise Manager – Business Development
Shelly Siu, Merchandise Manager – Product Development

*Design and Art Direction* Lynn Chin Nyuk Ling
*Photography* Edmond Ho, Jambu Studio
*Text and Recipe Testing* Violet Oon

Reprinted 2007

Published by Marshall Cavendish Cuisine
An imprint of Marshall Cavendish International
1 New Industrial Road, Singapore 536196

Marshall Cavendish is a trademark of Times Publishing Limited

National Library Board Singapore Cataloguing in Publication Data

Naturally Peninsula - Flavours. – Singapore : Marshall Cavendish Cuisine, c2007.
p. cm.

ISBN-13 : 978-981-261-375-2
ISBN-10 : 981-261-375-7

1. Cookery, International.

TX725.A1    641.59 -- dc22
SLS2006040254

Printed by Times International Printing

*Naturally Peninsula*
"To live well is to eat well"